NOTABLE
NORTH CAROLINA
WOMEN

NOTABLE NORTH CAROLINA WOMEN

by

Jennifer Ravi

Cover Design by Lynn Michelle Blanche

Winston-Salem, North Carolina

First Printing, April, 1992

Library of Congress Catalog Card Number 92-70165

ISBN 1-878177-03-6

Bandit Books, Inc.
P.O. Box 11721
Winston-Salem, NC 27106
(919) 785-7417

Printed in the United States of America

For Mom and Dad

TABLE OF CONTENTS

FOREWORD

When I moved to North Carolina almost three years ago, I began hearing about notable women associated with this state. Ava Gardner, Elizabeth Dole, Dolley Madison, Maya Angelou, and, of course, Frances Bavier became household names for me. Later I was working on a project for the Thelonious Monk Institute to bring professional jazz musicians into the public schools. During that time, I was amazed to find out Roberta Flack and Nina Simone were also North Carolina natives.

Shortly after that discovery, I had a conversation with a friend of mine, Jennifer FitzSimons, who had started a publishing company. We had tossed around a lot of ideas for writing projects before she started the company. Then one day she called with some more project possibilities. I listened to some of these but heard only "North Carolina women." Within minutes we agreed I would do the book.

Composed of biographies of 31 accomplished women connected with the state by birth or residence, this book is intended as an introduction. In compiling this list, I searched for unwavering criteria for inclusion but found that achievements rarely fall into neat categories. I wished for the time and luxury to research and write about all of the women I read about or was introduced to by friends, librarians, and women's studies professors; unfortunately, I was not so lucky. This is not an exclusive list, but it is a place to start.

The group I chose is an amalgamation of women from different social and economic classes, races, and professions. Some were born and lived their entire lives in the state. Others lived here for only a while. Each left an indelible mark on the state—and country as well. Some of their lives and stories are heart-rending, others mesmerizing, and others somewhat humorous or intriguing, but all have proved to be most inspiring.

Thanks to the numerous librarians who have assisted me, in particular those at the Winston-Salem Main Library North Carolina Room, and UNC Chapel Hill North Carolina Collection Library. The help of iconographic archivists at the state archive and Chapel Hill university archive is appreciated. Thanks also to those people who helped with research, gathering photographs, and setting up interviews. Also, Carla Lang, Jeff Blackie, Glenn and Noys Burchette, and Joe Wu.

A special thanks to Lynn Blanche for her cover design. Her friendship, support, and willingness to help have been invaluable gifts. Jennifer FitzSimons, my editor, gave me the freedom to write my manuscript and defended my deadline extensions; Barry McGee, my publisher, provided similar support and patience. To both I offer my profuse thanks.

My husband, Russ Parker, provided continued faith in the project, frequent nudges to get back to work, and invaluable editorial feedback for which I am very grateful.

NOTABLE NORTH CAROLINA WOMEN:
BRIEF DESCRIPTIONS

Annie Lowrie Alexander was the first woman to practice medicine in the South. Born and raised in Cornelius, she practiced in Charlotte.

Maya Angelou, who gained international acclaim for her writing on the black experience, has been Reynolds Professor of American Studies at Wake Forest University in Winston-Salem since 1981.

Penelope Barker gained notoriety for her leadership of the "Edenton Tea Party" in 1774. She lived in Edenton her entire life.

Frances Bavier starred as Aunt Bee in the television series *The Andy Griffith Show*, winning an Emmy in 1967 and a following which continues to this day. She retired to Siler City in 1972.

Anne Bonney was a pirate who raided ships in the North Carolina sounds in the 1700s.

Charlotte Hawkins Brown was a pioneer in education and race relations in North Carolina and established the Alice Freeman Palmer Institute in Sedalia.

Lillian Exum Clement became the first woman elected to the North Carolina state legislature.

Virginia Dare was the first English child born in colonial America. She was born on Roanoke Island in Dare County.

Susan Dimock became the first woman from North Carolina to practice medicine. She was a doctor in Massachusetts.

Dorothea Dix lobbied for the establishment of separate hospitals for the mentally ill. Dorothea Dix Hospital in Raleigh is named in her honor.

Elizabeth Hanford Dole was named Secretary of the Department of Transportation in 1983, making her the highest ranking woman in the U.S. government. She is a Salisbury native.

Gertrude B. Elion won the Nobel Prize for medicine in 1988. She is now a scientist emeritus for Burroughs Wellcome in Research Triangle Park.

Donna Fargo, born and raised in Mount Airy, won widespread attention in 1972 with the release of the hit single, "The Happiest Girl in the Whole U.S.A." which led to a Grammy.

Roberta Flack is an accomplished singer, pianist, songwriter, and arranger, whose hits include the 1973 release, "Killing Me Softly with His Song." She was born in Black Mountain and later taught in Farmville.

Inglis Fletcher wrote a series of historical novels which chronicled 200 years of North Carolina history.

Ava Gardner, famous for her acting as well as her personal life, was born and raised near Smithfield.

Kathryn Grayson, born in Winston-Salem, is a singer and actress who starred in many lavish musicals of the 1940s and early 1950s.

Elizabeth Duncan Koontz, the first black president of the National Education Association, was born and raised in Salisbury.

Flora MacDonald was a Scot who gained fame by aiding the escape of Bonnie Prince Charlie in 1746. She later spent a few years in North Carolina.

Dolley Payne Madison, the wife of President James Madison and White House hostess, was born and raised in Guilford County.

Shannon Ravenal edited *The Best American Short Stories* for 13 years. She is currently editorial director for Algonquin Books of Chapel Hill.

Susie Marshall Sharp was the state's first female city attorney and female superior court judge. She was also the first woman in U.S. history to be elected to head a state judicial system.

Nina Simone is a singer and pianist who gained widespread recognition with her 1959 recording of "I Love You Porgy" from Gershwin's *Porgy and Bess*. Her repertoire includes folk, gospel, jazz, and popular material. She was born and raised in Tryon.

Mary Martin Sloop was a physician who worked in a difficult rural area, Avery County. She and her husband developed the Crossnore School.

Kate Smith was a radio personality and patriotic symbol renowned for her rendition of "God Bless America." She lived in Raleigh the last seven years of her life.

Lee Smith is the author of several novels and short story collections, many of them set in or near the Appalachian Mountains.

Frances Fisher Tiernan was best known by her pen name, Christian Reid. She was North Carolina's most prolific novelist during the Reconstruction Period.

Anne Tyler is the author of 12 novels, including *The Accidental Tourist*, and has won the Pulitzer Prize for literature. She lived in North Carolina for several years.

Elizabeth P. Valk was recently named publisher of *Time* magazine. The Winston-Salem native is the first woman to hold that position.

Maggie Axe Wachacha is a Cherokee Indian who has served her people in western North Carolina as a healer and clerk for many years.

Anna McNeill Whistler was made famous by her son, James, one of the greatest American 19th century painters. She was born and reared in Wilmington.

POPULAR CULTURE

Anne Bonney
Courtesy of the North Carolina Division of Archives and History

Anne Bonney
circa 1700

While many women of her time gave in to traditional roles, Anne Bonney was not one of them. She earned a reputation as a tough pirate.

Born and raised in Ireland, she was the illegitimate daughter of an attorney (whose name is not known) and his maid. Their affair was scandalous. When Anne was a child her father's wife left him. Anne's mother, the maid, was fired. To cover his indiscretion, the attorney later dressed his daughter as a son, claiming that "he" was a relative's child who was going to be apprenticed into the law practice.

When Anne's father's wife blew the lid on this scheme, his wealthy mother stopped subsidizing him. He decided to take back the maid and they lived together openly. This caused more scandal and he lost his law practice.

As a result, he sailed for "Carolina" with Anne and her mother. Records are unclear as to whether they settled in North or South Carolina. It is believed this took place circa 1700.

When Anne's mother died, the daughter became mistress of her father's plantation. He had plans underway for a secure future for her, including marriage to a suitable gentleman and a good dowry.

However, Anne was not one to settle for such a life. Instead, she fell in love with a pirate by the name of James Bonney. They soon married and subsequently moved to Jamaica, where the pirating life continued. Anne's father promptly disinherited her.

About this time, the government of England, in an effort to recoup the money it was losing to pirate ships, offered a pardon to all pirates who would surrender themselves and change their evil ways.

James Bonney not only gave himself up but went a step further by ratting on his fellow pirates. Disgusted, Anne left him and took up with pirate captain, Calico Jack Rackham, who got his nickname because he always wore striped calico pants. Anne became his mistress.

While on board, Anne Bonney disguised herself as a male pirate. Of the 50 or so men on board, the only one privy to her secret was Captain Jack.

Later Anne Bonney and a Mark Read became very close. Rackham threatened the two of them, since he knew Bonney's secret. Rackham then learned that Mark was actually Mary, another woman assuming male identity. Rackham promised not to tell their secrets and the threat was diffused. Whether or not Mary and Anne had a relationship is not known, though it is suspected.

The Jamaican governor, who was tired of losing merchandise, commissioned a merchant ship to capture the pirates who were destroying commerce throughout the West Indies.

It wasn't long before the captain of the commissioned ship came upon Rackham's ship. As the story goes, the pirate men were drunk and stayed below refusing to put up a fight, whereas Mary and Anne climbed on deck and drew swords and guns.

The commissioned ship fired a cannon at the pirate ship, toppling one of its masts down onto Anne Bonney, who was knocked unconscious. Disgusted at their refusal to fight, Mary Read fired her pistols into the group of pirates, killing one and wounding Rackham in the leg. The other crew boarded Rackham's ship and easily captured the pirates.

The men were tried and hanged. Anne Bonney and Mary Read pleaded their "bellies" (pregnancy) and escaped the gallows. Bonney died in jail of fever and Read vanished without a trace.

SOURCES
The Pirates of Colonial North Carolina, pamphlet, 16th printing, pgs. 23-24, Hugh F. Rankin, Division of Archives and History, North Carolina Department of Cultural Resources, Raleigh, NC, 1989.
Asheville Citizen-Times, Asheville, NC, April 18, 1954, Robert H. Bartholomew, North Carolina Collection clipping file through 1975, University of North Carolina at Chapel Hill Library.
Cape Fear Friday Star-News, Wilmington, NC, July 4, 1975, unattributed, North Carolina Collection clipping file through 1975, University of North Carolina at Chapel Hill Library.
The News and Observer, Raleigh, NC, November 19, 1967, Mary Regan, North Carolina Collection clipping file through 1975, University of North Carolina at Chapel Hill Library.

Virginia Dare
1587-unknown

Virginia Dare is probably one of the most famous North Carolina "women" in the sense of name recognition, yet there are no accomplishments to bolster her popularity, and the simple fact of whether she lived much beyond infancy has never been ascertained.

Dare's claim to fame is that she was the first English person born in the New World. Although this makes her noteworthy, her story might not have become so popular had her existence not been shrouded in mystery. She disappeared from sight soon after her birth.

Dare's parents, Ananias and Eleanor White Dare, were part of an expedition that came to Roanoke Island in July of 1587. The couple made the trip from England because

Eleanor's father, John White, had already made three voyages to Virginia, and since women as well as men were wanted for this expedition, he encouraged his daughter and son-in-law to come with him on yet another voyage.

The expedition, sponsored by Sir Walter Raleigh, was supposed to establish a settlement in the Chesapeake Bay area, but the captain of their ship landed instead on Roanoke Island.

The new colonists found something wrong soon after their arrival. The 15 men who were left on Roanoke Island from the previous expedition were found murdered by Indians.

Virginia Dare was born about a month after the colony landed. The only facts known about Dare's life are that she was christened on the following Sunday and that she was the first child born in Virginia, and consequently named Virginia.

The Baptism of Virginia Dare
by William Steene
Courtesy of the North Carolina Division of Archives and History

At that time North Carolina was in the territory designated as Virginia.

Shortly after their arrival, many of the new colonists wanted John White to sail to England to get more supplies for the colony. He did this, but when White reached England,

he found his country was at war with Spain, and there was no ship he could use for his return voyage. Consequently, it was three years before he was able to return to his colony.

It is unclear what happened during those three years; it has become a matter for speculation and research. When White finally arrived on March 20, 1590, no greeting party or grand ceremony met him, simply silence and the word "CROATOAN" carved on a post. He found no one from the colony he'd left, including his daughter, son-in-law, and granddaughter. To this day their disappearance remains a mystery.

The state of North Carolina named a county after the young British subject; Dare County commemorates her birthplace.

One of the explanations for the disappearance of "The Lost Colony" is that they went to live with the Indians on either Hatteras or Ocracoke Island. Another is that they went to live with a tribe of Indians in Robeson County; this tribe uses many words from Old English and has many folk tales which would seem to connect them to White's colony.

SOURCES
Biographical History of North Carolina from Colonial Times to the Present, Volume Four, pgs. 8-18, edited by Samuel A. Ashe, Charles L. Van Noppen Publisher, Greensboro, NC, 1908.

Tar Heel Women, Lou Rogers, Warren Publishing Company, Raleigh, NC, 1949.

Dictionary of American Biography, Volume Three, pgs. 73-74, edited by Allen Johnson and Dumas Malone, Charles Scribner's Sons, New York, 1958.

Flora MacDonald
1722-1790

Flora MacDonald lived only briefly in North Carolina, but she brought with her the celebrity of her adventures.

Born in 1722 on an island in the Hebrides off the coast of Scotland, she lost her father in infancy. When she was six, her mother was abducted and married by Hugh McDonald. Flora's brother took care of her until she was 13 when she was taken to live with relatives and taught by a family governess.

During a visit with other relatives in South Uist, Flora became a central player in a real life historical drama.

Charles Edward, the Stuart pretender to the Crown of England, had decided to challenge the current ruling family, the Hanovers. He suffered a devastating loss at the Battle of Culloden on April 16, 1746. A search was made for him and a reward offered for his capture.

The "Bonnie Prince" or "younger pretender" as he was often called, escaped to South Uist where Flora was staying.

Flora MacDonald
Courtesy of the North Carolina Collection, UNC at Chapel Hill Library

Someone suggested that Edward be disguised so he could flee the country in safety. He was dressed as Flora's maid-in-waiting, and together they made it to France.

The Bonnie Prince escaped, but Flora was not as fortunate. She was captured and imprisoned in Scotland and later in the Tower of London. She became a heroine of sorts. No evidence against her was produced and she was released in accordance with the Act of Indemnity in 1747. The Bonnie Prince made his way to Italy where he died in 1788.

Four years after her return to Scotland, she married Allan MacDonald, son of the Laird of Kingsburgh, who had inherited his father's estate as well as his title. Through her marriage to MacDonald, she became mistress of the same house in which the Bonnie Prince slept during his first night on the Isle of Skye, June 29, 1746, after his escape from Uist.

The house and bed became quite an attraction. When Dr. Samuel Johnson, author of *Dictionary of the English Language*, toured the Hebrides with his friend, James Boswell, in 1773, he slept in the same bed.

Flora MacDonald's connection to North Carolina began at this point. Many Europeans were immigrating to the New World because of the economic possibilities there, and MacDonald and her husband followed suit, sailing to North Carolina in 1774. When they arrived in Wilmington, a ball was given in her honor.

The MacDonalds lived at Cameron Hill in Cumberland and at Cross Creek for about a year. In 1776, her husband purchased a tract of land, then in Anson County, now on the borders of Richmond and Montgomery counties, called "Killiegray" and they moved there.

At the same time, her husband received a commission to keep the Scots in their area loyal to the British Crown. Flora accompanied her husband on horseback, calling the Highlanders to be loyal to their king.

During the Revolutionary War, her husband was captured at the Battle of Moore's Creek on February 27, 1776. He was imprisoned in Halifax jail. He told her to return to Scotland, which she was able to do in 1779.

On the voyage, Flora's ship encountered a French warship. She displayed her characteristic fearlessness and inspired the passengers with her courage. The attack was repulsed, but Flora broke her arm in the struggle.

It was this experience which elicited her comment, "I have hazarded my life for the House of Stuart and the House of Hanover, and I do not see that I am a great gainer by either."

She died at Kingsburgh on March 5, 1790. She was buried at Bilmuir Cemetery with many mourners in attendance. The sheets on which the Bonnie Prince had lain formed her shroud.

A women's college in Red Springs, Robeson County, carried her name for many years. It is now part of St. Andrews Presbyterian College in Laurinburg.

SOURCES
Dictionary of North Carolina Biography, Volume Four, Maud Thomas Smith, pgs. 138-139, edited by William S. Powell, The University of North Carolina Press, Chapel Hill, NC, 1991.
Biographical History of North Carolina from Colonial Times to the Present, Volume Seven, pgs. 292-296, edited by Samuel A. Ashe, Charles L. Van Noppen Publisher, Greensboro, NC, 1908.
Tar Heel Women, Lou Rogers, Warren Publishing Company, Raleigh, NC, 1949.

Dolley Madison
Courtesy of the North Carolina Division of Archives and History

Dolley Payne Madison
1768-1849

Dolley Payne Madison achieved popularity and regard largely through the work she did for her husband, President James Madison. Hers was not a time when women were free to explore careers and interests as they are today.

Dolley Payne was born in Guilford County to Quaker parents. As Lou Rogers points out in her short biography of Madison, "Dolly (sic) may have been born in a log house and have grown up in the simplicity of a Quaker home but that certainly does not mean that she was not well-born or well-trained. Dolly's mother was Mary Coles of Hanover County, Virginia, and was courted by Thomas Jefferson, Alexander Hamilton, Aaron Burr, and many others famous in American history."

Her father, John Payne, was opposed to slavery and freed all of his slaves in 1782. The following year the family moved to Philadelphia, the nation's capital at the time.

In 1790, Dolley married John Todd, a Quaker lawyer. She gave birth to two sons, and the family lived comfortably.

But in the summer of 1793, yellow fever spread throughout their area. Todd sent his wife and young sons to Gray's Ferry on Schuylkill River, not far from Philadelphia, hoping they would not contract the disease. Todd returned to Philadelphia to tend to his parents who had become ill with the fever. Todd himself became sick and died. Dolley also fell ill and didn't awaken until about a month later, to learn the news of her husband and youngest son's deaths.

In 1794, she met James Madison, often referred to as "The Father of the United States Constitution." He was 43 and she was 26. Rogers says he was "a conventional suitor but an ardent one, and was prodded on by George and Martha Washington, who were very fond of him." They married that year. Dolley was expelled from the Society of Friends because her new husband was not a Quaker.

For the rest of her life Dolley Madison led a high profile existence, hosting many political and social functions. In

1801, President Thomas Jefferson named James Madison secretary of state. As Jefferson and his vice-president, Aaron Burr, were both widowers, Dolley became Jefferson's acting hostess, and was quite good at receiving guests.

It has frequently been observed that this work helped her husband's political career enormously. In 1809, James Madison was elected the fourth president of the United States. Dolley Madison continued to create a social and political life that was highly popular and quite helpful to her husband.

During the War of 1812, she packed, removed, and saved the Cabinet papers, as well as a Gilbert Stuart portrait of George Washington, shortly before the British burned the presidential mansion. After the blackened walls were painted white to help conceal the damage, the presidential home became known as the White House.

At the end of Madison's second term in 1817, it was said that Dolley Madison was the most popular person in the United States. The couple retired to their home in Montpelier, Virginia, where she worked on her husband's papers and entertained a constant flow of visitors from home and abroad.

After her husband's death in 1836, Dolley Madison returned to Washington, where she was almost as popular as she had been during her time as First Lady.

SOURCES
Dictionary of North Carolina Biography, Volume Four, pgs.
199-200, Ethel Stephens Arnett, edited by William S. Powell,
The University of North Carolina Press, Chapel Hill, NC, 1991.
Tar Heel Women, Lou Rogers, Warren Publishing Company,
Raleigh, NC, 1949.
Mrs. James Madison, The Incomparable Dolley, Ethel
Stephens Arnett, Piedmont Press, Greensboro, NC, 1972.

Anna McNeill Whistler
1804-1881

Anna McNeill Whistler is the woman made internationally
famous by her son, James, in the painting entitled *Whistler's
Mother*. The image of a somber-looking woman seated in
profile has been reproduced on everything from greeting
cards to candy boxes; it was even reproduced as a Mother's
Day stamp in 1934.

Born in Wilmington on September 27, 1804, Anna McNeill
was the fifth child of Daniel McNeill and Martha Kingsley.
She was raised in a genteel fashion. Evangelical Protestant-
ism was elemental as well in her upbringing.

She married George Whistler, a major in the army, when
she was 27. Trained as a civil engineer, he turned to the more
lucrative business of building railroads, and the family moved
to Lowell, Massachusetts.

Upon her marriage, Anna Whistler assumed the care of

George's three children from a previous marriage: George, Joseph, and Deborah. She gave birth to five sons, three of whom died of illness.

During much of the marriage, the family moved around or else the father was away on business. One such move was to Russia for five years where George Whistler had been invited by Czar Nicholas I to help build a railroad between Moscow and St. Petersburg.

When George Whistler died of cholera in 1849, Anna Whistler returned to the U.S., settling in Connecticut with her sons James, "Jemie," and William, "Willie."

She got Jemie into West Point, but he preferred socializing with friends and drawing to following regimens, and was finally dismissed. Willie wanted to become a doctor, but wasn't accepted into Columbia, so he went to work in a machine shop in Baltimore. He later went to Philadelphia Medical School, finishing in 1860.

One of Anna Whistler's best friends was Thomas Carlyle, the English essayist and historian. The image of his mother seated by the fire next to Carlyle left a lasting impression on James Whistler, who was to become one of the greatest 19th century American painters.

The portrait of his mother, originally titled *A Portrait in*

Black and White, first sold for $620. The painting now hangs in the Louvre in Paris, and is insured for over $1 million.

SOURCES
Biographical Dictionary of Famous Tar Heels, pg. 118, edited by Richard Cooper, Creative Productions, Raleigh, NC, 1988.
Tar Heel Women, Lou Rogers, Warren Publishing Company, Raleigh, NC, 1949.
Art in America, November, 1984, pgs. 138-151, Phoebe Lloyd.
Greensboro Daily News, April 11, 1948, Theresa Thomas.

EDUCATION

Charlotte Hawkins Brown
Courtesy of the North Carolina Division of Archives and History

Charlotte Hawkins Brown
1883-1961

The granddaughter of former slaves, Charlotte Hawkins was born in Henderson, and gained her fame by making lasting contributions to the education of Blacks and to race relations.

She was born to Edmund and Caroline Hawkins on June 11, 1883, 20 years after President Lincoln issued the Emancipation Proclamation abolishing slavery. When Charlotte was six, her mother and stepfather moved the family to Cambridge, Massachusetts where she completed elementary and secondary school.

A chance meeting with Alice Freeman Palmer, the second president of Wellesley College and wife of a Harvard professor, was to prove invaluable to the young Hawkins.

Charlotte frequently told the story of being employed as a baby-sitter for a family in Cambridge. One day while taking the child for a stroll, she had a copy of *Virgil* in hand. This mix of commonplace and highbrow in the young girl attracted the attention of Palmer, who took an immediate interest in her. Palmer paid for Hawkins to attend the State Normal School of Salem, Massachusetts.

In 1901, the 18 year-old Hawkins returned to North Carolina to teach southern Blacks through the American Missionary Association. She taught at a rural black school at Bethany Congregational Church in Sedalia, Guilford County.

The school closed after one term, but Hawkins decided to remain in the community and establish her own school. A year later, she founded the Palmer Institute, named in honor of Alice Freeman Palmer, her friend and chief benefactor.

The school evolved from a small neighborhood elementary school to a high school and then to a junior college targeted to the sons and daughters of the black elite business and professional classes.

In 1911, on the day after her 29th birthday, Charlotte Hawkins married Edward S. Brown. Her husband helped with the teaching and administration of the school, but did not find the challenge he needed. Feeling that the school was more his wife's project than his own, Edward Brown left to work at a similar school in South Carolina. Although the couple corresponded, they never got back together and eventually divorced.

Charlotte Brown continued to improve the Palmer Institute. She had neither the staff nor expertise in marketing that colleges and universities rely on today for fundraising. However, it is said that she raised as much as $1 million from wealthy friends in the North and South.

Brown also became known for her work in race relations. She gave frequent speeches at colleges, churches, and women's associations, and belonged to numerous interracial organizations.

In the fall of 1920, an incident occurred which radicalized her. She was on board a Pullman car from Greensboro to Memphis, Tennessee, where she was to attend a women's interracial meeting. When she left her sleeping compartment the next morning to sit in the coach area, she was confronted by 12 large white men who forced her to move to the "Negro coach."

Brown was understandably humiliated, but the indignation was not over. She was marched through three cars, including one which had Southern white women on the way to the same interracial meeting, "where they declared their purpose was to make the Negro woman unashamed and unafraid," she was later quoted as saying.

She sued the Pullman Company and obtained a settlement, though her attorney suggested she let it go. She responded by saying "a few of us must be sacrificed...in order to get a step ahead." Brown was a leading promoter of equal opportunities for Blacks and an advocate of integrated schools.

Brown retired from the office of president of the school in 1952, but she remained as the director of finance until 1955. She died in 1961 in Greensboro. Ten years later, the doors to the Palmer Institute were closed.

Today what remains is the spirit left from those 1000 students who graduated from the institute and a North Carolina State Historic Site in Sedalia, which was opened to the public in 1987. It is located at the old Palmer Institute site and is the first site honoring a black person in North Carolina. It includes exhibits, and plans are being made for a black history resource center.

BOOKS
The Correct Thing To Do, To Say, To Wear, 1941

SOURCES
Journal of Negro Education, Vol. 51, No. 3, 1982, Howard University, "Charlotte Hawkins Brown," Sandra N. Smith and Earle H. West, Winston-Salem Main Library North Carolina Room clipping file.
Charlotte Hawkins Brown Memorial State Historic Site brochure, Division of Archives and History, Department of Cultural Resources, North Carolina Historic Sites, undated.
Dictionary of North Carolina Biography, Volume One, pgs. 242-243, A.M. Burns III, edited by William S. Powell, The University of North Carolina Press, Chapel Hill, NC, 1979.
The Lengthening Shadow of a Woman; A Biography of Charlotte Hawkins Brown, Constance H. Marteena, Exposition Press, Hicksville, NY, 1977.

Elizabeth Duncan Koontz
1919-1989

Elizabeth Duncan Koontz came from a family of educators. Her father was a high school principal, her mother was an elementary school teacher, and several of her six siblings held jobs with schools or colleges.

Koontz worked as a special education teacher at Price Junior-Senior High School in Salisbury, but this was not to be her claim to fame. Her most noteworthy contributions to education included service as president of the National Education Association in 1968, director of the Women's Bureau of the Department of Labor in 1969, and delegate to the United Nations Commission on Working Women.

Koontz was the first black president of the NEA, at the time the highest federal position ever held by a black woman.

After graduating from Price High School in Salisbury, she studied English and elementary education at Livingstone College, receiving a B.A. in 1938.

Her first teaching assignment was in Dunn with the Harnett County Training School, a black school, where she was given a special education class. She later referred to it as "the kind of class that should never be given to beginning teachers but always is. I resented the fact that people felt these children couldn't learn. But it was a challenge to me. I'd seen my mother work with illiterates and I'd seen them learn. I guess we were all sort of taught to take up for the underdog."

After a couple of years, she went to Atlanta, Georgia, where she studied at Atlanta University, taking an M.A. in elementary education in 1941. She later did graduate work in elementary education at Columbia and Indiana Universities, and in special education at North Carolina State College at Durham.

In 1945, she joined Price Junior-Senior High School, a black school in Salisbury. Two years later she married Harry L. Koontz, mathematics instructor and athletic director at Dunbar High School in East Spencer.

Elizabeth Koontz

Courtesy of J.Y. Joiner Library, East Carolina University

Elizabeth Koontz became quite active in the NEA in 1952, after the association's North Carolina chapter modified its traditional racial policy which had excluded Blacks from any participation. During the next ten years, she moved from the local to national level in responsibility within the organization.

In 1962, North Carolina Governor Terry Sanford named Koontz to his Commission on the Status of Women. President Lyndon B. Johnson appointed her to the National Advisory Council on the Education of Disadvantaged Children in 1965.

She was elected president of the NEA in July 1967, and took office a year later at the association's 106th annual convention in Dallas, Texas.

In her speeches in 1968, she called on teachers to join together to ease racial tensions in the schools and to change educational bureaucracies, outmoded methods and curricula, and inadequate budgets, including those for teachers' salaries.

In an interview in *Look* (September 3, 1968), Koontz said, "The public rendered us sterile. We never talked about salaries, even though every other profession was demanding more money. Education was left way behind because those who should have been fighting for education were told it was less than professional to do so. Then we teachers were blamed for bad schools because we remained silent."

She garnered the label "militant" but wore it with pride, saying, "We have to be militant, but it is not militancy without responsibility. It involves a new determination to accept the responsibility we should have accepted long ago."

President-elect Richard Nixon appointed Koontz director of the Women's Bureau of the Department of Labor in 1969, a position she held until 1973. Always willing to speak her mind, her ideas included recognizing the labor of women who stay at home providing domestic services by giving them Social Security.

From 1973 to 1975, she was coordinator of the nutrition programs for the North Carolina Department of Human Resources. In 1975, she was named the assistant state school superintendent, a post she held until she retired in 1982.

She died on January 6, 1989 at her home in Salisbury.

SOURCES
Current Biography Yearbook 1969, editor Charles Moritz, The H.W. Wilson Company, New York, 1969.

The News and Observer, Raleigh, NC, July 28, 1968, Bebe Moore, North Carolina Collection clipping file through 1975, University of North Carolina at Chapel Hill Library.

The News and Observer, Raleigh, NC, January 15, 1969, Rose Post, North Carolina Collection clipping file through 1975, University of North Carolina at Chapel Hill Library.

Greensboro Daily News, September 15, 1974, Joe McNulty, North Carolina Collection clipping file through 1975, University of North Carolina at Chapel Hill Library.

Dr. Mary Martin Sloop
1873-1962

Mary Martin Sloop's story is one of old-fashioned American ingenuity and perseverance. Born and reared in Davidson, she made her name in Avery County where she worked with mountain inhabitants as a doctor, teacher, and missionary.

Mary spent many of her early years at Davidson College where her father was a faculty member. She attended a one-teacher school in Davidson until she was 15. Then she was sent to Statesville Female College for Women, from which she graduated in 1891 at the age of 18.

Her mother became ill and Mary spent 12 years taking care of her. At the same time she secretly began taking pre-med courses. Mary studied French, a feminine subject, so her mother wouldn't guess her true aspirations.

Early on Mary had been inspired by two guests who had

The two Doctors Sloop often operated outside, here under an
"antiseptic" apple tree
Courtesy of the North Carolina Division of Archives and History

visited her family, Dr. and Mrs. McGilvary. The two were missionaries to Siam and spoke movingly about the need for missionaries who were trained physicians. Mary had also developed a love for teaching, which she showed through her religious education of the cook's children.

After her mother's death, Mary began preparation as a medical missionary. She took her first year of medical studies at Davidson, but they refused to let her study anatomy and she was forced to transfer to another institution.

She wrote in her book, *Miracle in the Hills*, "It wasn't considered proper at all for me to go into a dissecting room with all those naked cadavers lying about on the dissecting tables! That indeed would have been highly unladylike. The neighbors would have never recovered from the shock of hearing about it."

Mary enrolled in the Women's Medical College of Pennsylvania, from which she was graduated. Afterward she applied to work as a missionary in Africa, but her application was refused, so she interned for a year at the New England Hospital for Women and Children. Then she became the first resident physician at Agnes Scott College in Georgia.

During her medical studies at Davidson, she renewed her friendship with Eustace Sloop, who was also a medical student. After they both completed their training, they were married in Blowing Rock and began a life of medical mission work in the area of the state they both loved.

She knew the region well as her father had built the family's first summer home at Blowing Rock when she was a child. She had also spent a lot of time with the mountain people. Dr. Eustace Sloop began a small practice in Plumtree.

Drs. Sloop helped the inhabitants in many aspects of their lives; they doctored, taught Sunday school, worked on building projects, and even lobbied for roads.

The Sloops established the very successful Crossnore School. Built bit by bit through the resale of donated clothing, they cleared more than $1,000 the first year, enabling the school to enroll four girls. By 1924, about 12 years later, they cleared $10,000. Crossnore went from being a one-room school of four students to a nine-month school with trained teachers.

"One of the finest things about our boys and girls is that after going out to finish their education, as many of them do, they usually come back to work among their own people as teachers, ministers, nurses, etc.," Mary Sloop said.

She said her plan for Crossnore was to provide the young women with alternatives. At that time, the practice was to marry in the early teens and settle into a domestic life of cooking, cleaning, and raising children. Women were considered old maids at 16.

In 1951, Mary Sloop was named American Mother of the Year. In 1953, she wrote *Miracle in the Hills*, an account of the Sloops' work at Crossnore.

BOOKS

Miracle in the Hills, Mary T. Martin Sloop, M.D. with Legette Blythe, McGraw-Hill Book Company, Inc., New York, 1953.

SOURCES

Miracle in the Hills, Mary T. Martin Sloop, M.D. with Legette Blythe, McGraw-Hill Book Company, Inc., New York, 1953.

The Country Gentleman, "The Country Gentlewoman," March 14, 1925, Winifred Kirkland, North Carolina Collection, University of North Carolina at Chapel Hill Library.

Charlotte Observer, August 23, 1936, Mrs. J. A. Yarbrough, North Carolina Collection clipping file through 1975, University of North Carolina at Chapel Hill Library.

POLITICS

*TOP: The North Carolina House of
Representatives of 1921
LEFT: Lillian Exum Clement*

Courtesy of the North Carolina Division
of Archives and History

Lillian Exum Clement
1894-1924

Lillian Exum Clement gained her fame as the first woman in the North Carolina state legislature, but the years leading to that point were simple and filled with hard work.

She was born near Black Mountain, the sixth child of George W. and Sarah Elizabeth Burnette Clement.

Clement attended a one-room school in Black Mountain until her early teens when her father moved the family to Asheville, where he was helping to build George Vanderbilt's Biltmore House. There she attended the All Souls Parish School and later the Normal and Collegiate Institute and Asheville Business College.

Clement knew early she wanted a career. She once said to a brother, "Mankind has written millions of laws for thousands of years to enforce only eight fundamental ones. I am going to study law."

Clement did not enter the legal profession the traditional way, not that there was any traditional way for women at that time. She began her career working in a sheriff's office as a deputy under three sheriffs. In the evenings she studied law, first with J. J. Britt and then with Robert C. Goldstein. In 1916, she passed the bar examination along with about 70 other students, many of whom had studied at universities and colleges.

Judge Thomas A. Jones presented her with a bouquet of carnations and welcomed her into the profession. He was the first to call her "Brother Exum," a name that was to stick with her throughout her legal career.

On February 2, 1917, in Room 15 in the Law Building

near the old Buncombe County Courthouse, L. Exum Clement hung her sign, becoming the first woman in North Carolina to begin the practice of law without the "legitimacy" of male partners.

Over the next four years, she earned a reputation as a shrewd and able criminal lawyer. However, in spite of the support she received, she quickly realized she had to fight the idea that being a woman attorney was somehow a contradiction in terms.

With ratification of the 19th Amendment in 1920, women's suffrage was underway. At this time, Brother Exum was approached by the Democratic Party to run for representative from Buncombe County to the North Carolina state legislature. She surprised everyone by agreeing to run as she was not a suffragette. The Democrats backed her all the way.

The *Asheville Citizen-Times* wrote, "What faith these men displayed in Exum Clement's ability, how revolutionary the choice of a woman candidate in those troubled times, what a shock to the nation when a Southern Gentlewoman was elected over her male opponent by a landslide victory of 10,368 votes to 41, the largest majority ever polled in the state up to that time, and—most remarkable of all—elected in an entirely male ballot."

On her first day in the House of Representatives she told a reporter from the *Raleigh News and Observer*, "I was afraid at first that the men would oppose me because I am a woman, but I don't feel that way now. I have always worked with men, and I know them as they are. I have no false illusions or fears of them...I am by nature, very conservative, but I am firm in my convictions. I want to blaze a trail for other women. I know that years from now there will be many other women in politics, but you have to start a thing."

Those who expected her to sit quietly, observe, and otherwise be unobtrusive were quite mistaken. She introduced 17 bills in the general assembly. Sixteen are now laws which, in one way or another, benefit the lives of those who live in the state.

Her bills included the establishment of private voting booths and a secret ballot, tuberculin testing of dairy herds and sanitary barns, and a reduction in the number of years of abandonment from ten to five to decree a divorce.

Clement married Eller Stafford, a staff writer for the *Asheville Citizen*, during the third month of her term in the assembly. The general assembly, unaccustomed to having women as members, found it necessary to enact a special law so her name could be changed for the roll call. She was then known as Mrs. E. E. Stafford.

She did not run for public office again; however, she was director of the State Hospital at Morganton and a founder of the Asheville Business and Professional Women's Club.

She died in 1924 and was buried in the Clement family plot in Riverside Cemetery in Asheville.

SOURCES
Asheville Citizen-Times, May 8, 1960, North Carolina Collection clipping file through 1975, University of North Carolina at Chapel Hill Library.
Biographical Dictionary of Famous Tar Heels, pgs. 22-23, edited by Richard Cooper, Creative Productions, Raleigh, NC, 1988.

Elizabeth Hanford Dole
1936-

Elizabeth Hanford Dole figured out at a young age what she was good at and has lived her life taking on one challenge after another.

Dole's name came into the household vocabulary when President Ronald Reagan named her Secretary of Transportation in 1983, making her the highest ranking woman in the U.S. government. But this success was merely one in a long line.

Dole was born Mary Elizabeth Hanford in Salisbury. In an article in *The Saturday Evening Post* she described it as "still the kind of place where people tip their hat in welcome and conversations start with a friendly 'Hey.'"

Her successes came early. In the book she co-wrote with her husband, Senator Robert Dole, *The Doles: Unlimited Partners*, she writes of earning straight A's and writing prize-winning essays. Her political aspirations began when she was elected president of the bird club in the third grade.

She applied to only one university, Duke, "for the simple reason that my brother, who I still have on a pedestal, had gone there."

In her first letter home from Duke, she announced that she was thinking of majoring in political science, saying, "I think it would be fascinating to learn about American government, history in the making."

Dole was a member of the Delta Delta Delta sorority at Duke and its May Queen of 1958. She was also the student government president for Duke's Women's College. She graduated with distinction.

Elizabeth Dole
Courtesy of Elizabeth Dole

After graduation, she attended Harvard University, where she received a master's degree in government and education.

Then she attended Harvard Law School, where she was one of 15 women in a class of 550. She was president of the Marshall Law Club, president of the Harvard International Law Club, and assistant editor of the International Legal Studies Bibliography Project. She graduated in 1965.

During the years she was doing graduate work, Dole worked as a North Carolina senator's aide. She also worked for the United Nations in New York, beginning as a tour guide and ending up in the general secretariat's office.

After completing her education, Dole moved to Washington, D.C., where she began work as a staff aide in the Department of Health, Education, and Welfare.

Dole then took the position of Deputy Director of the U.S. Office of Consumer Affairs, serving under Presidents Lyndon Johnson and Richard Nixon. During this time, she began her dedication to public safety, which earned her the National Safety Council's Distinguished Service to Safety Award in 1989.

In 1973, she was named a member of the U.S. Trade Commission, a position she held for five years.

In 1975, she married Senator Robert Dole of Kansas and supported his political ambitions in three failed bids for higher office; vice-president in 1976, and Republican candidate for president in 1980 and 1988.

In 1983, President Reagan named her Secretary of the Department of Transportation. She was the first woman to hold that position.

Some of her safety initiatives included: the adoption of new regulations increasing the production of automobiles with air bags and automatic safety belts, leading a crusade against drunk driving, and overhauling the aviation safety inspection process.

In 1989, President George Bush appointed Dole to the position of Secretary of the Department of Labor, where she worked for two years. She was noted particularly for her dedication to safety in the workplace, improving relations between labor and management, upgrading the skills of American workers, and the training and education of "at-risk" youth.

Dole is currently president of the American Red Cross, overseeing a staff of 23,000 and over a million volunteers. On her first day in the position, Dole said that volunteers were the "heart and soul" of the organization, and announced that she would be a volunteer and accept no salary during her first year as president.

The organization provides emergency communications to U.S. armed forces; collects, processes, and distributes over half of the nation's blood and blood products; responds to natural disasters such as floods, fires, and earthquakes; and has instructed over nine million Americans in health and safety courses.

She is often mentioned as a future candidate for high national office.

BOOKS
The Doles: Unlimited Partners, 1988.

SOURCES
The Saturday Evening Post, May/June 1990, "Labor's Elizabeth Dole," pgs. 44-49, Diane Bartley.
McCall's, May 1990, "A Loving Daughter's Tribute," pgs. 53-54, Elizabeth Dole.
Press information from Elizabeth Hanford Dole.

Susie Marshall Sharp
1907-

Susie Marshall Sharp is one of a select few North Carolina women who, in her lifetime, achieved some kind of first. In fact, throughout her life she achieved several such distinctions.

She was the only woman in her class at the University of North Carolina Law School; she was the first woman appointed judge to a North Carolina superior court; she was appointed the first woman associate justice on the North Carolina Supreme Court; and in 1974, she was promoted to chief justice, the first woman elected chief justice of a state supreme court in the United States.

Sharp was the oldest of seven children born to Jim and Annie Sharp. She grew up in Rocky Mount, Stoneville, Madison, and Reidsville, and graduated from Reidsville High School.

Sharp did her undergraduate studies at the North Carolina College for Women in Greensboro. Upon graduation, she enrolled at the University of North Carolina at Chapel Hill. She was the only woman in a class of 61. She was student editor of the North Carolina Law Review and was made a member of the Order of the Coif, the most highly prized of all the law school fraternities in the country.

She passed the bar at the end of her first year at Chapel Hill. She continued taking classes and began assisting her father, an attorney, with research and preparation for court cases. The work included arguing a case before the North Carolina Supreme Court in 1929, at the age of 21. She lost the case, but made headlines.

Susie Sharp

Courtesy of the North Carolina Division of Archives and History

After graduating from law school in 1929 with honors, her father made her a full partner, and they became Sharp and Sharp, Attorneys-At-Law. The partnership, based in Reidsville, lasted 20 years. They took cases all over Rockingham and surrounding counties.

At the age of 30, in 1937, Sharp was named city attorney of Reidsville, becoming the first female city attorney in the state's history.

In 1949, North Carolina Governor W. Kerr Scott named Sharp Superior Court judge, the first woman to hold that position in the state's history of more than 170 years. In that capacity, she presided over court all over the state. Several governors reappointed her to the position.

In 1962, Governor Terry Sanford appointed Sharp associate justice of the North Carolina Supreme Court. In 1974, she was elected chief justice. It was the first time in U.S. history a woman was elected to head a state judicial system.

Sharp was not the first woman to serve as a state's chief justice. A member of Arizona's highest court held that distinction, Associate Justice Lorna Lockwood. The judges on the Arizona court rotate in the chief's position, primarily a ceremonial one. No other woman, though, has ever been elected to the post. Sharp functioned as spokesperson for and director of the North Carolina judiciary.

While on the supreme court, Sharp voted against reinstating a mandatory death penalty, upheld the state's right to use funds for busing school children in urban areas, and ruled against the use of state bonds for private industrial development.

In 1976, *Time* included her in a cover piece entitled "A Dozen Who Made a Difference," a feature on the significant contributions of a select group of living women. Sharp said, "Women lawyers aren't a curiosity any more, but I was a curiosity in my little town."

Sharp, who has never married, said that while some women may be able to balance a career and a family, she was not one of them. "The trouble comes when a woman tries to be too many things at one time: a wife, a mother, a career woman, a femme fatale. That's when the psychiatrist is called in at umpteen dollars an hour. A woman has to draw up a blueprint. She has got to budget her life."

Judge Sharp retired in 1979. She currently lives in Raleigh.

WORKS
author of more than 600 opinions

SOURCES
Time, January 5, 1976, pgs. 19-20.
Susie Marshall Sharp, First Woman of Justice, Richard Cooper, Creative Productions, Raleigh, NC, 1985.
Greensboro Daily News, November 7, 1974, North Carolina Collection clipping file through 1975, University of North Carolina at Chapel Hill Library.
The News and Observer, Raleigh, NC, August 20, 1974, North Carolina Collection clipping file through 1975, University of North Carolina at Chapel Hill Library.
The News and Observer, Raleigh, NC, July 15, 1979, North Carolina Collection clipping file, unbound, University of North Carolina at Chapel Hill Library.

PUBLISHING

Maya Angelou
Courtesy of Maya Angelou—Credit: © Tim Richmond/Katz Pictures

Maya Angelou
1928-

Maya Angelou, writer, singer, actress, and teacher, is currently Reynolds Professor of American Studies at Wake Forest University in Winston-Salem. Accomplished in many areas, Angelou's literature has gained her the widest acclaim. Not only is it praised for its celebration of the black experience; it inspires the reader to creatively transform life's experiences, good and bad, rather than merely survive them.

Although her greatest renown has come to Angelou for her writing, it is singing and dancing which started her career. Ironically, Billie Holiday had prophesied this years before.

In June of 1948, according to an article in *The Atlantic Monthly*, Angelou was singing in a nightclub and settled into a house in Laurel Canyon, in the Hollywood Hills.

Her voice coach set up a meeting with Billie Holiday. The two met, and the normally raucous and wild Holiday softened in her stay with Angelou, spending time with Angelou's son Guy and enjoying a home cooked meal. As Holiday was leaving, she told Angelou, "You're going to be famous, but it won't be for singing."

In 1954 and 1955, Angelou appeared in a production of *Porgy and Bess* which toured 22 countries.

But by the time she was 30, she had made the commitment to become a writer. She moved to Brooklyn to learn her craft and be near her friend, John Killens, activist and author. Through weekly meetings of the Harlem Writers Guild, Angelou learned to treat her writing seriously. "If I wanted to write, I had to be willing to develop a kind of concentration found mostly in people awaiting execution. I had to learn technique and surrender my ignorance." She was accepted as a practicing member by a group of established writers that included James Baldwin.

I Know Why the Caged Bird Sings, her first autobiographical book which was published in 1970, chronicles the early years of her life in the 1930s and 1940s with her grandmother in Stamps, Arkansas, and with her mother in St. Louis and San Francisco. Angelou eloquently and evocatively describes her unique experiences, telling the story of the coming of age and struggles of a young, poor black girl in the Old South. The book speaks to the cohesiveness of the black community and church, and the force of racism and its various faces.

In her second autobiography, *Gather Together in My Name*, she describes leaving for San Diego and her mother's admonition to "Be the best of anything you get into. If you want to be a whore, it's your life. Be a damn good one."

Singin' and Swingin' and Gettin' Merry Like Christmas recounts her successful dancing career. She tells of her experience on a European tour with the cast of *Porgy and Bess*.

The Heart of a Woman covers the era of civil rights marches both at home and abroad.

In *All God's Children Need Traveling Shoes*, Angelou recounts her experience with a group of black American expatriates in Ghana when that country won its independence.

In 1971, Angelou returned to the South after a self-imposed hiatus. "I stayed out of the South intentionally for almost 30 years because of the negative memories. The first time I came to Winston-Salem in 1971, I had not been (in the South) since...1946. I just didn't feel like crossing into areas where I was certain to be insulted or hurt in some way."

What she found, she says, were people she liked a great deal, black and white. In an article in *Ebony* she said, "I knew that morning, that one day, I would return to the South in general, and North Carolina in particular. I would find friends, join a church, and add my energy to the positive movement to make this country more than it is today. More than what James Baldwin calls 'these yet to be United States.' And I have done so."

Returning to the place that had haunted her before was yet another opportunity to go beyond the hurt and anger of injustice, and create something positive, fresh, and productive. Asked if she's had any reservations about her return, Angelou replies she regrets nothing. "Life is so capricious and there's such a sense of humor required to live...I do my work a lot, pray a lot, and try to laugh as much as I cry."

BOOKS
I Know Why the Caged Bird Sings, 1970
Just Give Me a Cool Drink of Water 'Fore I Diiie, 1971
Gather Together in My Name, 1974
Oh Pray My Wings are Gonna Fit Me Well, 1975
Singin' and Swingin' and Gettin' Merry Like Christmas, 1976
And Still I Rise, 1978
The Heart of a Woman, 1981
Shaker, Why Don't You Sing?, 1983

SOURCES
Telephone interview with Maya Angelou on January 2, 1992.
Ebony, January 1982, pgs. 130-134, "Why I Moved Back to the South," Maya Angelou.
Dictionary of Literary Biography, Volume 38, Afro-American Writers After 1955: Dramatists and Prose Writers, edited by Thadious M. Davis and Trudier Harris, A Bruccoli Clark Book, Gale Research Company, Detroit, 1985.
The Atlantic Monthly, September 1990, pg. 61, Nancy Caldwell Sorel.

Inglis Fletcher
1879-1969

Inglis Fletcher was a Southerner by temperament. Born in Illinois, her genealogical researches, focused on North Carolina, pulled her back to the state of her ancestors and led to a career as a chronicler of the state's history.

After graduating from the School of Fine Arts of Washington University in St. Louis, Missouri, she planned to become a sculptress. This changed when she married mining engineer, John George Fletcher. His work required that they move frequently. They lived in Alaska, Washington, and California, which she later chronicled in her autobiography *Pay, Pack and Follow.*

The couple lived in San Francisco from 1925 to 1938. During that time she operated a lecture bureau, presenting celebrities including the writer, Will Durant.

One of her first attempts at serious writing was a novel about a freeholder in Alaska, but she destroyed the manuscript when the publisher returned it for revision. It was her only unpublished book. She said:

> It was a book about Alaska. On the urging of a friend I had sent it to a publisher. The manuscript came back to me along with a several-page letter suggesting revision. I read the letter through in dismay, laid it aside and proceeded to forget about it. One day in a fit of housecleaning I found the manuscript and threw it into the wastebasket. Months later I happened to run into the publisher. 'Say,' he asked, 'when are we going to have your book? Have you finished the revision yet? We have been looking for it.' There was

nothing for it but to tell him the truth. That was my first book, the one I wrote to throw away.

In 1928, she took a seven month trip to British Central Africa. She spent three years writing a novel, which was based on the life of her guide in Africa. *The White Leopard* was published in 1931 as a Junior Literary Guild Selection

Inglis Fletcher at work at Bandon Plantation
Courtesy of the North Carolina Division of Archives and History

for older boys. That book was quickly followed by another in 1932. *Red Jasmine*, an adult novel, was set in a colonial African town and was semi-autobiographical.

Not long after the publication of her second novel, she stumbled onto some information which would lead her to a lifelong pursuit. At the Huntington Library in Pasadena, California, she came upon some tantalizing passages in the

Colonial Records of North Carolina, which mentioned her Tyrell County ancestors. She went back day after day. This was the beginning of her work chronicling the evolution of the state of North Carolina.

She visited North Carolina in 1934 and 1937 to research *Raleigh's Eden*. Other research included six years of examining hundreds of documents, papers, books, and reports, including materials in London.

The result was the historical novel, published in 1940, which recounts North Carolina between 1765 and 1782, focusing on the plantation families of Albemarle as they faced the events of the Revolution. *Raleigh's Eden* was the first of a twelve-volume series on North Carolina's early years. The series has been praised for its meticulous detail. In the novels, historical figures frequently mingle with fictional ones, while still maintaining historical accuracy.

In 1944, the Fletchers moved to Bandon Plantation on the Chowan River, near Edenton. In a twist of fate, the house had been owned by one of the characters in *Raleigh's Eden*. This character is said to have indirectly caused Richard Chapman, Inglis Fletcher's ancestor, to move to Illinois.

Fletcher worked steadily on the Carolina Series for the next 24 years. She wrote five and a half days a week, beginning in the morning when she would go to her study and sit at her table "as methodically as any plow hand takes to the fields with his mule." Some days she didn't even put a syllable to paper, but once she wrote 18,000 words without stopping. Mr. Fletcher would blow a whistle for quitting time. He claimed this was his contribution to her novels.

Fletcher claimed Sir Walter Scott as a major influence on her work. She also wrote, "I cannot remember any time when I did not write or want to write. It is my firm belief that when one has the creative impulse, plus imagination, it is impossible not to write."

She died in 1969.

MAJOR WORKS
The White Leopard, A Tale of the African Bush, 1931
Red Jasmine, A Novel of Africa, 1932
The Carolina Series
Raleigh's Eden, 1940
Men of Albemarle, 1942
Lusty Wind for Carolina, 1944
Toil of the Brave, 1946
Roanoke Hundred, 1948
Bennett's Welcome, 1950
Queen's Gift, 1952
The Scotswoman, 1955
The Wind in the Forest, 1957
Cormorant's Brood, 1959
Wicked Lady, 1962
Rogue's Harbor, 1964

SOURCES
Inglis Fletcher of Bandon, Bobbs-Merrill, 1946, North Carolina Collection, University of North Carolina at Chapel Hill Library.
North Carolina Authors: A Selective Handbook, pgs. 38-39, Prepared by a Joint Committee of the North Carolina English Teachers Association and the North Carolina Library Association, 1952, University of North Carolina at Chapel Hill Library.
Dictionary of North Carolina Biography, Volume Two, pgs. 207-208, Richard Walser, edited by William S. Powell, The University of North Carolina Press, Chapel Hill, NC, 1986.

Shannon Ravenal
Courtesy of Shannon Ravenal—Credit: Tim Richmond

Shannon Ravenal
1938-

Shannon Ravenal gained recognition for editing 13 volumes of Houghton Mifflin's series, *The Best American Short Stories*. Originally from North Carolina, her work as editor for Algonquin Books of Chapel Hill has finally brought her back home.

Born in Charlotte, she lived there until she was five. From the time she was eight until she left for Hollins College, she lived in Charleston, South Carolina.

When Ravenal entered publishing out of college, it was with little thought toward "a career," though she was bright, competent, and eager to learn. She attributes her early interest in the business to two disparate sources. One was Louis Rubin, a professor at Hollins College, who encouraged her to edit the student literary journal.

The other was the movie *The Best of Everything*. As Ravenal tells it, the movie, based on a book by Rona Jaffe, starred Joan Crawford "as the executive bitch editor" and Hope Lange as the recent college graduate. Lange whizzes through days of what takes most people years, if they are lucky. She gets the job her first day of looking, finds a manuscript the second, and marries the author on the third or fourth.

Though she laughs easily at the silliness of it now, it's clear that the glamorous image had an appeal for the young Ravenal. And so upon graduating cum laude from Hollins with a B.A. in English Literature in 1960, she headed for New York, the publishing mecca. She took a position as advertising copy writer with Holt, Rinehart, & Winston for a year, writing direct mail.

It was an exciting time. She lived in New York City with four other girls. They socialized with a group of Southern boys who were friends. She refers to them as the "Southern Mafia," explaining that in New York, the tendency was to stick with one's own, and part of that had to do with her background. "I grew up as a Ravenal in a very phony sort of aristocratic lineage oriented society, which I wasn't aware of until I left," she says.

But the chance to be on her own was something Ravenal yearned for, and so she moved to Boston and took a job at Houghton Mifflin as secretary of the trade division. "Those were the old days when girls didn't go very far in publishing. It was a very old boy organization, but I had these two women (editors who were her bosses) who had made it, and they were very receptive to my efforts."

She was promoted to senior editor within three years, and then became editor of the trade division from 1964 until her resignation in 1971. In 1968, she married Dale Purves, when she was "just under 30." Many of her friends had married the day after they left Hollins, she says, adding "I didn't set out to be a career person at all, it just happened." Her plans were to live in Boston and "marry the right person in Charleston." But she was never able to break away from the job.

She had to resign when she was seven months pregnant because of company policy. She said it was a big shock to find that she didn't really want to be at home. So she eventually went back as a reader.

Ravenal moved around with her husband, now the chairman of the Department of Neurobiology at Duke University, along the "science circuit" to London, St. Louis, and Chapel Hill. She worked as a freelance consultant to Houghton Mifflin, edited a scientific journal, and began teaching creative writing at the college level.

Through all the moves there were some constants. In 1977, when Martha Foley died, Ravenal took over editing *The Best American Short Stories*. She did so until 1990. The annual anthology, established in 1915, is very well regarded.

In 1982, she joined her former teacher, Louis Rubin, in establishing Algonquin Books of Chapel Hill (now a division of Workman Publishing Company). At that time she also began editing *New Stories from the South*. She moved back to North Carolina in 1990 and currently serves as editorial director for Algonquin.

Ravenal has been a juror and panelist for many organizations including The REA Award for the Short Story and the National Endowment for the Arts. In 1990, The Council of Literary Magazines and Presses gave her its Distinguished Achievement Award.

MAJOR ACCOMPLISHMENTS
The Best American Short Stories, series editor, 1977-1990
New Stories from the South, editor, 1982-
Editorial Director, Algonquin Books, 1991-

SOURCES
Telephone interview with Shannon Ravenal on July 18, 1991.
Biographical information from Shannon Ravenal.

Lee Smith
1944-

Lee Smith, widely acclaimed for capturing the language and atmosphere of the people in the Appalachian Mountains, has been a resident of Chapel Hill since 1974.

In the *New York Times Book Review*, Katha Pollitt said, "Hers is a South divested of mystery, of broodings about hellfire and race and fatal family history...It is a South of football games and miniature golf courses, of chain stores and the go-getting Rotarians who manage them, of tract homes on streets with names like Country Club Circle. Her heroines get their ideas from women's magazines and soap operas, and if they are very daring, from Phil Donahue."

Smith was born in Grundy, Virginia, to Ernest Lee and Virginia Smith. "It was wonderful. It was a very small town. My father ran the dime store, which he still does (at 83); my grandfather was county treasurer...for 46 years; Uncle Jack ran the grocery store...It was the most secure place in the world to grow up," she says.

Her parents had been married for 18 years when Lee was born. She was an only child, though she had lots of cousins and relatives around. And her parents were "endlessly in-volved" in her activities.

As long as she can remember, she wanted to be a writer, even as a little girl. She wrote books and sold them to neighbors and had her own newspaper. In one of these books she described her two favorite people—Adlai Stevenson and Jane Russell. The two head west in a wagon, and then the unlikely couple convert to Mormonism.

Her early schooling was in Grundy. She studied with local kids, most of whom were from poor families. "We had nothing

Lee Smith
Courtesy of Lee Smith

of the sense of social classes. The only difference among the people was where you went to church...There were no black people in the county," she says.

For high school she went to St. Catherine's, a private preparatory school for girls in Richmond, Virginia. "Looking back at it now, (it) seems a really bizarre thing to do." She didn't know anyone who had gone away for school. "It just wasn't the sort of thing people did at that time," she recalls.

She thrived in a disciplined environment, but it also made her different. "From the point I went to St. Catherine's, I was a split person in a way," she says. At St. Catherine's all the girls were going to college, and all had interests that were different from the girls with whom she had been a cheerleader in Grundy.

"Ever since I went off to school, I have been very aware of that conflict. Am I a mountain girl who's going to live here (Grundy) or am I going off and do things? (This is) thematically real important in what I've written," she says, "because it raises questions like: Can you ever go home when you have become more educated?" It took her years to get enough distance to be able to return to it in her writing.

After St. Catherine's, she attended Hollins College, a women's college, graduating in 1967 with a B.A. in English. It was a place where she excelled. She struck up friendships with women and men who had similar interests, including Henry Taylor, a Pulitzer Prize winning poet, and writer Annie Dillard.

She wrote prolifically while she was at Hollins and felt the professors created a nurturing environment, sharing their work and reading student's work with loving eyes. All this went on without the constant distraction of boys.

"I was just so crazy about boys. We still had plenty of dates on the weekends," she says. But she voices uncertainty as to whether she would have felt so free to explore her interests at a larger co-ed university.

She wrote stories, worked on a literary journal, and edited

the yearbook. She also wrote a novel as an independent study, which became her first published novel and won her a Book-of-the-Month fellowship.

She has written professionally ever since, but it has never been in the way that many dream of writing—alone, with the ability to set one's own hours and not worry about money. She has had a family, and has held other jobs to make ends meet.

She married poet James E. Seay in 1967, and has two children, Josh and Page, from that marriage. In 1985, she married journalist Hal Crowther.

"There's this enormous tension all the time. If you're writing, you should be doing something else...Life seems to be full of conflict. I love to be in the middle of things. I would never have traded it for anything. I would never not have children...(they have) opened up my life to a lot of feelings that I never would have had access to. And husbands are the same way...I think you ought to sort of jump in there with both feet."

Her work has included reporting and teaching at several institutions such as Duke University and the University of North Carolina at Chapel Hill. She is currently an associate professor in the English Department at North Carolina State University.

NOVELS

The Last Day the Dogbushes Bloomed, 1968
Something in the Wind, 1971
Fancy Strut, 1973
Black Mountain Breakdown, 1981
Cakewalk, 1981
Oral History, 1983
Family Linen, 1985
Fair and Tender Ladies, 1988
Me and My Baby View the Eclipse, 1990

SOURCES

Telephone interview with Lee Smith on August 5, 1991.

Biographical information from Lee Smith.

Dictionary of Literary Biography Yearbook: 1983, Katherine Kearns, edited by Mary Bruccoli and Jean W. Ross, Gale Research Company, Detroit, 1984.

Contemporary Authors, Vol. 119, edited by Hal May, Gale Research Company, Detroit, 1987.

Frances Fisher Tiernan
"Christian Reid"
1846-1920

Few writers have made as financially successful a career as Frances Fisher Tiernan. The daughter of a well-placed Salisbury family, she started writing at an early age to entertain herself and family members. Several years later her mother died. Then her father was killed in battle during the Civil War, leaving three children without parents or a source of income.

At nineteen, Frances and her two siblings went to live with their aunt, Christine Fisher, in Salisbury. Kind and generous, her aunt had lost her fortune as well. Frances came up with the idea of writing for a living. Her family was amused at the idea, but she persisted, choosing Christian Reid as her pseudonym because it didn't bring up the question of gender at a time when it was easier to be a male writer.

Frances Fisher Tiernan
(Christian Reid)
Courtesy of the North Carolina Division of Archives and History

Her first book, *Valerie Aylmer*, published in 1870, sold 18,000 copies. For the next nine years she wrote several short stories and novels of Southern life. *Morton House* is considered one of her best works from this period. *The Land of the Sky*, which depicts life in western North Carolina, also gained recognition, and the phrase is now commonly used to describe that part of the state.

Her contributions as a writer were recognized far beyond the bounds of North Carolina. She was the first Southerner—man or woman—to receive the Laetare Medal for distinction in letters from The University of Notre Dame in 1909. She was also made a member of an exclusive French society, The Order of the Golden Rose, after her story, "The Lady of Las Cruces," was translated into French.

She married James Tiernan in 1887. After the marriage, the couple moved to Mexico, where he had purchased mines. They lived there for the next 20 years. Her writing from this period includes: *Carmela*, *The Picture of Las Cruces*, and *The Land of the Sun*.

She returned to Salisbury in 1897 because of her husband's ill health. He died six months later, at which time she told her publishers she could never write again. She wrote poems for herself at the time and helped organize book clubs.

Tiernan did write again, though. One of her works was *Under the Southern Cross*, a play about the War Between the States. At her death, her work consisted of more than forty novels, short stories, odes, and poems.

SELECTED BOOKS
Valerie Aylmer, 1870
Morton House, Ebb-Tide and Other Stories, 1872
Nina's Atonement and Other Stories, 1873
A Summer Idyl, 1878
A Comedy of Elopement, 1893
The Picture of Las Cruces, 1896
Princess Nadine, 1908

SOURCES

North Carolina Authors: A Selected Handbook, prepared by a Joint Committee of the North Carolina English Teachers Association and the North Carolina Library Association, 1952, University of North Carolina at Chapel Hill Library.

Tar Heel Women, Lou Rogers, Warren Publishing Company, Raleigh, NC, 1949.

The News and Observer, Raleigh, NC, October 30, 1927, Dr. Archibald Henderson, North Carolina Collection clipping file, University of North Carolina at Chapel Hill Library.

Anne Tyler
1941-

Anne Tyler, who has published 12 novels in the past 27 years, won a Pulitzer Prize, and has written numerous short stories, lived in North Carolina for several years and attended Duke University.

She gained widespread attention with the film, *The Accidental Tourist*, which starred William Hurt and Kathleen Turner. Adapted from her 1985 novel, it is the story of a travel writer who despises traveling, preferring to remain in the confines of his home. This novel is typical of her writing which focuses on quirky characters living simple, everyday lives.

While she has captured the imagination of many readers,

Anne Tyler the person has become somewhat of an enigma. For the past eleven years, she has shunned talk shows and interviews, the traditional staples for authors who want to sell their books. She has also been fortunate enough to be able to make that choice and continue a productive and successful career.

What is known about Tyler is that she lives on a quiet, tree-lined street in Baltimore, Maryland with her husband, Taghi M. Modaressi, a psychiatrist. She has two college-age daughters.

She was born in Minneapolis, Minnesota on October 25, 1941 to Lloyd Parry Tyler, a chemist, and Phyllis Mahon Tyler. She has lived in the South most of her life, particularly in North Carolina and Maryland. Until she was about 11, she lived with her parents in several communes.

In one interview in 1980, she said that those experiences

Anne Tyler
Courtesy of Knopf—Credit: © Diana Walker

made her look "at the normal world with a certain amount of distance and surprise, which can sometimes be helpful to a writer."

She attended high school in Raleigh, and at 16, entered Duke University. It was there she met Reynolds Price, the North Carolina novelist and short story writer. He had attended her high school and was becoming established as a novelist. He referred her to his agent, Diarmuid Russell.

After graduating from Duke with a B.A. in Russian Studies, she pursued that interest through graduate work at Columbia University for a year. She worked as the Russian bibliographer at Duke from 1962 to 1963, and then as assistant to the librarian at McGill University in Montreal, Canada from 1964 to 1965.

She married Modaressi in 1963, and two years later they had a daughter, Tezh. Their second child, Mitra, was born in 1967.

Tyler wrote her first novel, *If Morning Ever Comes*, in 1964, during the first six months of her marriage when she was unemployed. She followed it up with *The Tin Can Tree* and several other novels. Writing became her career.

Tyler's work has been compared to that of Eudora Welty, her favorite writer. Tyler said many years ago that reading Welty taught her there were stories of meaning and value in the everyday life about her.

And that is the area in which she excels. Her novel, *Breathing Lessons*, is a study of an older married couple. The setting of the entire novel is a weekend in which the couple is driving from North Carolina to Maryland for a funeral. But in that short weekend, Tyler weaves a narrative of great complexity and intensity, including the wife's frustration with her husband and how she almost had an affair. By the end of the novel, this very human relationship is somehow stronger, a testimony to the strength and vitality of marriage.

In one interview, Tyler stated she never intended to become a writer, that she would have liked to have been an artist and still toys with the notion of becoming a book illustrator.

NOVELS
If Morning Ever Comes, 1964
The Tin Can Tree, 1965
A Slipping Down Life, 1970
The Clock Winder, 1972
Celestial Navigation, 1974
Searching for Caleb, 1976
Earthly Possessions, 1977
Morgan's Passing, 1980
Dinner at the Homesick Restaurant, 1982
The Accidental Tourist, 1985
Breathing Lessons, 1988
Saint Maybe, 1991

SOURCES
Dictionary of Literary Biography, Volume Six, American Novelists Since World War II, Second Series, Mary Ellen Brooks, edited by James A. Kilder, Jr., Gale Research Company, Detroit, 1980.
Contemporary Authors, Volume 11, New Revision Series, edited by Ann Evory and Linda Metzger, Gale Research Company, Detroit, 1984.

Elizabeth P. Valk
1950-

When Winston-Salem native Elizabeth P. (Lisa) Valk was named publisher of *Time* magazine in July 1991, it was another in a line of firsts for her. She was the first woman to be named as publisher for *Time*, *Life*, and *People*. Furthermore, with her appointment to *Time*, it is the first time the same person has been publisher of all three magazines.

Although Valk is quite comfortable with her role, she is candid in admitting that it was not the career she had planned when she was a child.

"I was fascinated by what Daddy did (internist at Bowman Gray School of Medicine in Winston-Salem), but it never occurred to me to go into medicine." Instead she says, "I was a slug. I wanted to sit around and read books." And when she thought of the future, it was in traditional terms. "My image of myself was to definitely be a mother and a wife."

Valk seems almost unaware of the significance her achievements have for many women. "Maybe why I've been gender blind is that I've been to school with women all my life. The thought that I would be shut out of something because I'm a woman never occurred to me."

Born and raised in Winston-Salem, she attended Summit School, a private elementary school where she won the academic award for her class each year she was there. She attended high school at St. Timothy's, a private boarding school for girls in Maryland. She received a bachelor's degree in political science from Hollins College, a private women's institution, in Virginia.

Upon graduation she married a medical student and moved to Boston in 1973, settling into a traditional lifestyle.

She divorced in 1975, and took a job at Massachusetts General Hospital, though she couldn't type and refused to budge on that point.

She was at "Mass Gen" four years, which was excellent experience in managing traffic in an inpatient clinic. She was responsible for coordinating activities as the unit secretary. "I loved it. It was a real challenge to try to induce all these people to do the things I wanted them to do, with no real authority."

She enjoyed the job and thrived, but realized the people who were moving up all had M.B.As. So at 27, she decided to get one. She was accepted into a program at Harvard. Describing her studies, she says, "I went to Harvard thinking I would go back into health care. I was a business illiterate."

Instead she flourished in marketing. She found she enjoyed the mix of creative and analytical skills required to solve real problems. "Marketing was something I really took to. It seemed natural. I just found that really interesting."

Upon graduation in 1979, she was recruited by Time Inc. With an interest in books and marketing, a position in circulation seemed like a good fit. She worked hard and quickly made her way up through the ranks of *Time* magazine, starting as a staff person and moving up to assistant circulation director.

Her career at Time Inc. has been a series of promotions and new challenges. In 1982, she became circulation director of *Fortune* magazine. Two years later, she was appointed to the same position at *Sports Illustrated*. Less than a year later, she was appointed circulation director of *Time* magazine.

In 1986, she was made publisher of *Life* magazine. She became a vice-president of the Time Inc. Magazine Company in August 1987. In October 1988, she was named publisher of *People* magazine, and in 1989, she was promoted to senior vice-president of the company.

Elizabeth P. Valk
Courtesy of Time Inc.

Asked what achievement she is most proud of, she quickly responds with, "I am very proud of the team I assembled at *People*. That was probably a model publishing team. I felt so good about the team. I felt that *People* magazine became a place where the best and brightest wanted to work—and did."

Though she is proud of her accomplishments, she describes herself as a "reluctant spokesperson for women." Congratulatory notes, such as one signed by "the working girls," touched her. "I never thought of myself as a pioneer...I always thought I was in over my head."

ACHIEVEMENTS

Publisher, *Life* magazine, 1986
Publisher, *People* magazine, 1988
Publisher, *Time* magazine, 1991

SOURCES

In-person interview with Elizabeth P. Valk on July 24, 1991.
Biographical information from *Time*.
Winston-Salem Journal, February 18, 1990, Bill Goodykoontz.
Winston-Salem Journal, December 28, 1986, Ken Otterbourg.

ENTERTAINMENT

Frances Bavier
Courtesy of the Frances Bavier Estate

Frances Bavier
"Aunt Bee"
1902-1989

Frances Bavier became famous for her role as Aunt Bee in *The Andy Griffith Show*, the sixties television series which portrayed small town life in the South. It conjured up images of salt of the earth, country folk with traditional values, both of which can be found aplenty throughout the state of North Carolina. The show was set in the fictional town of Mayberry, North Carolina, which was based on Griffith's hometown of Mount Airy. In the show Bavier played housekeeper to sheriff Andy Taylor. She was gentle, understanding, and very domestic.

But Bavier's real life experiences couldn't have been more different. Frances Bavier did not come from the country. She was born in New York City in 1902. She attended Columbia University and was a graduate of the American Academy of the Arts in 1925.

Before joining *The Andy Griffith Show*, she acted in numerous stage productions including stints in vaudeville and on Broadway where she appeared in such productions as *Kiss and Tell, Point of No Return*, and *Lady Says No*. During World War II, she toured Europe and the Pacific with the USO. *The Andy Griffith Show*, which ran from 1960 to 1968, and its sequel, *Mayberry, R.F.D.*, which ran from 1968 to 1971, proved to be her longest engagement and made her into a cult figure. In 1967, she won an Emmy for her role as Aunt Bee.

When she retired in 1972, she chose Siler City as her home. She had participated in a diet at Duke University and met a woman whose sister she later visited in Siler City. She said she enjoyed the town and was seeking a quiet life like the one she had helped to portray in the series.

In 1973, she spoke to members of the North Carolina Writers Conference. She compared the writing of *The Andy Griffith Show* to that of a short story, noting that in some episodes the writing was perfect, with the script writer having to tell a complete story from start to climax to finish in a 20 minute time span.

At the same event, Bavier said few actresses ever become truly great in their field when compared with male actors, with the exceptions of Dame Sybil Thorndyle and Dame Judith Anderson. When asked if she thought that would change, she said she thought men approached acting as they might a job of engineering and most women didn't have the interest in being so methodical or in being anything except women.

In another interview that same year, she admitted she watched reruns of the show almost every night. She also said her attraction to Siler City was mixed. She was attracted to the small town atmosphere and friendliness, yet she was a professional actress who spent most of her life working and little time creating a traditional family life.

She grew impatient when people stopped to chat, brought her cookies, or offered to mow her lawn, as often happened. Many of her neighbors and those who came on pilgrimages to meet "Aunt Bee" had difficulty separating "Aunt Bee" from Frances Bavier the person.

In 1981, she said, "After (life in) New York and Hollywood, I was convinced, yes, go ahead, move. But they (Siler City residents) don't know me. Their life experiences are different from mine. And I'm always looked at as someone who has money. But Siler City is no different from anywhere. That's what happened to America. The world is different now."

She died at her home, which she shared with 15 cats, at the age of 86 on December 7, 1989. She had no known living relatives.

SOURCES
The Andy Griffith Show, Richard Kelly, John F. Blair, Publisher, Winston-Salem, NC, 1981.
Winston-Salem Journal, Associated Press, December 8, 1989.
The Pilot-Southern Pines, Southern Pines, NC, August 1, 1973, unattributed, North Carolina Collection clipping file through 1975, University of North Carolina at Chapel Hill Library.
Durham Morning Herald, February 18, 1973, Kathy McPherson, North Carolina Collection clipping file through 1975, University of North Carolina at Chapel Hill Library.
The News and Observer, Raleigh, NC, May 17, 1981, Curtis Austin, North Carolina Collection clipping file, unbound, University of North Carolina at Chapel Hill Library.
The State, January 1990, pg. 3, unattributed.

Donna Fargo
1949-

Donna Fargo, the singer who cascaded into the limelight with the country hit, "The Happiest Girl in the Whole U.S.A.", was born and raised in Mount Airy.

Born Eliza Yvonne Vaughn, her father grew tobacco near Mount Airy and her mother worked the third shift at a sock mill in town. At Mount Airy High School she was named homecoming queen her junior year. The following year she was the head cheerleader and named the most spirited and popular girl in her class. She also sang in the Slate Mountain Baptist Church when she was growing up.

After graduation she attended High Point College, where she was graduated with a bachelor's degree in English. She moved to Los Angeles, where she taught high school English in the nearby town of Covina, California.

At an audition in Hollywood, she met Stan Silver, the record producer. He was impressed with her vocal talent and became her producer. Silver and Fargo later married.

Although she had no formal musical training, Silver encouraged her to learn and play guitar and to write songs. She recorded three singles and performed live while teaching full-time.

In 1972, she wrote "The Happiest Girl in the Whole U.S.A." and the same year, *Billboard* magazine named her "Best New Female Artist." She also received a Grammy, an award from the Country Music Association, and a platinum album (one million copies sold). She quit her teaching job that June, and the following fall she moved to Nashville, Tennessee.

The next four years included the hits: "Funny Face," "You Can't Be a Beacon," "It Do Feel Good," and "Don't Be Angry."

From 1972 to 1978, Fargo experienced periodic numbness, loss of coordination, and fatigue. After filming her television show, *Donna*, in 1978, she checked into the Sansum Medical Clinic in Santa Barbara and was diagnosed with multiple sclerosis. She was told there was no cure for the disease.

"What do I do if I can't continue my career," she asked her doctor. "You go on," he replied.

Fargo turned to the Bible and spirit-building tapes for strength and comfort. She recounted her experience for the *Los Angeles Herald Examiner*: "I had this beautiful room where you looked out and saw the ocean, and I just tried to find myself spiritually. And I began believing there was hope. I started working on that, and I think faith is something you have to work on. As it says in the Bible, faith comes by hearing, and hearing comes by the word of God. That means you need to read the Bible and read faith-building mater-

Donna Fargo
Courtesy of Donna Fargo

ial...It just really saved my life, because if you're not thinking right you can readily hurt yourself, especially with this, because it's so easy to get depressed. It's a physically depressing disease. And I'm thankful that I turned...inward. I think you have to approach it mentally, spiritually, and nutritionally. That's all you can do."

For a couple of weeks she was totally without feeling, unable to write her name, and barely able to walk. She went into physical therapy with her husband's support. As a result, she was able to regain much of her physical control.

In 1981, she recorded "Brotherly Love," her first recording of gospel music.

ALBUMS
The Happiest Girl in the Whole U.S.A.
Dark-Eyed Lady
Fargo Country
Just for You
The Best of Donna Fargo

SOURCES
The Country Music Encyclopedia, Melvin Shestack, Thomas Y. Crowell Company, New York, 1974.
The News and Observer, Raleigh, NC, October 19, 1980, "The Tar Heel of the Week," Bill Morrison.
Los Angeles Herald Examiner, April 21, 1980.
Winston-Salem Journal, September 25, 1988, Greg Hitt, North Carolina Collection, unbound, University of North Carolina at Chapel Hill Library.
Press Information from Donna Fargo.

Roberta Flack
1940-

Renowned pianist and vocalist Roberta Flack, spent her early years in North Carolina, and later returned to teach in Farmville.

Roberta was born in Black Mountain, one of four children of Laron and Irene Flack. Her father, a draftsman, taught himself to play the piano. Her mother, a domestic worker and cook, played the piano for the local black Methodist church.

Roberta loved music early on, and some of her earliest memories are from the local A.M.E. Zion Church. She said their music "didn't have the raunchy, wide-open, free, spontaneous, full-of-life thing you could hear at the Baptist Church down the street." So, whenever she could, she sneaked over to the Baptist Church to hear gospel singers such as Mahalia Jackson or Sam Cooke and The Soul Stirrers.

When Roberta was about five, the family moved near Washington, D.C. When she turned nine, she began taking piano lessons and listening to a wide range of popular music, R&B, jazz, blues, and pop.

Flack grew up in Arlington, Virginia. She studied from the age of 12 with Hazel Harrison, a concert pianist, and after only a year, placed second in a statewide contest for black students with her performance of a Scarlatti sonata. As a teenager, her musical interests were mainly classical.

She was a brilliant student, graduating from high school at the age of 15, at which time she began studies at Howard University on a full music scholarship. Within a year, she was conducting her sorority's vocal quartet; accompanying pop, jazz, and opera singers; had changed her major from

Roberta Flack
Courtesy of Roberta Flack

piano to voice; and was assisting the school's choir conductor. To earn extra money she also taught piano privately and played organ at her parents' church.

Flack then changed her major to music education, becoming the first black student teacher at an all-white school near Chevy Chase, Maryland. She began graduate studies in music, but the sudden death of her father forced her to leave both school and home and take a teaching job in Farmville, North Carolina to support herself.

Farmville was a big change. Flack describes it as "very segregated, very backward." She taught English and music to high school students. After one year, she moved to Washington, D.C., where she spent the next four years teaching at several junior high schools.

It was during this period that her professional music career began to take off. Flack was an accompanist to opera singers at the Tivoli Club in D.C. During intermissions she sang and played blues and folk songs and pop standards. When her voice teacher suggested she had a good future as a pop rather than classical musician, she began reshaping her repertoire, and her reputation spread. At one Capitol Hill club, Mr. Henry's, the upstairs was constructed with church pew seating, especially for her. Burt Bacharach, Carmen McRae, Woody Allen, Bill Cosby, Les McCann, Ramsey Lewis, and Johnny Mathis attended, as did many others. She often shared her stage with them. One night she even played with Liberace.

By the summer of 1968, Flack's reputation had grown enormously. Within days of seeing her perform, Les McCann arranged an audition for her with Atlantic Records. Only months later, *First Take*, her debut album, was cut and released, including "The First Time Ever I Saw Your Face."

A year later, she released her second album, *Chapter Two*, featuring the songs: "Do What You Gotta Do," "Just Like a Woman," and "The Impossible Dream." In 1971, she released *Quiet Fire*, and had the hit, "Will You Still Love Me Tomorrow?"

In 1972, "The First Time Ever I Saw Your Face" was included in Clint Eastwood's *Play Misty for Me*, and within weeks the single went to # 1. At the same time her fourth album was released, Washington, D.C. proclaimed Roberta Flack Day, a weekend celebration including receptions at the Kennedy Center and the Congressional Caucus Room.

Only a few weeks later, Atlantic released a new Flack single with Donny Hathaway, "Where is The Love." The album went gold in two weeks. The single remained in the Top 10 for two months straight, and also went gold. At the 1973 Grammy Awards, "First Time Ever" won Record of the Year and Song of the Year, while "Where is The Love" won Best Pop Vocal by a Duo. At the same time, "Killing Me Softly With His Song" was certified gold, and was both the # 1 pop and R&B song in the country.

At the '74 Grammys, "Killing Me Softly" won Record of the Year, Song of the Year, and Best Pop Vocal by a Female. The follow-up single, "Feel Like Makin' Love," went to # 1 on the pop, R&B, and easy listening charts. It became Flack's eighth million-seller in less than two and a half years. The album *Feel Like Makin' Love* was released in 1975, the first produced by Flack herself.

She did not release her next record, *Blue Lights in the Basement,* until December 1977. This is her personal favorite. A second collaboration with Peabo Bryson, *Born to Love,* was released in 1983 and created a stir with "Tonight I Celebrate My Love." She toured Japan and England, and sang "Goodbye Sadness" on Yoko Ono's tribute to her late husband, John Lennon, *Every Man Has a Woman.*

In 1986, she released a single rendition of "We Shall Overcome" to commemorate Martin Luther King's birthday. In 1988, Flack released the album, *Oasis,* which featured the work of David Sanborn, Marvin Hamlisch, Quincy Jones, and others. Her latest album is *Set the Night to Music,* featuring Maxi Priest.

"In the past few years since I recorded 'Tonight I Celebrate

My Love' with Peabo Bryson, I have been searching for the perfect combination of a number of elements that I think are necessary for a good record. You need a good song written by a wonderful writer, either to be sung by yourself or with someone who is extremely empathetic. You need the right people, the right songs, the right idea and concept for the album, and the right situations to put all of this together. I was able to combine them to create a piece of work which I think is (one) of my richest and most energetic. It represents a search in my creative life for the right place to rest, to be isolated, to be energized, and to come up with something that people would like...I didn't want just commercial songs, but ones that have some importance in my life, and actually define my existence."

ALBUMS
First Take, 1969
Chapter Two, 1970
Quiet Fire, 1971
Roberta Flack and Donny Hathaway, 1972
Feel Like Makin' Love, 1975
Blue Lights in the Basement, 1977
Roberta Flack Featuring Donny Hathaway, 1980
Live and More, 1980
The Best of Roberta Flack, 1982
Born to Love, 1983
Oasis, 1988
Set the Night to Music, 1991

SOURCES
Encyclopedia of Jazz, Leonard Feather.
Essence, February 1989, pgs. 52-126, "An Intimate Talk With Roberta Flack," Susan L. Taylor.
The News and Observer, Raleigh, NC, July 12, 1987, "The Tar Heel of the Week," Guy Munger.
Press information from Roberta Flack.

Ava Gardner
1922-1990

Ava Gardner won national attention as a film actress and as the wife of three notable entertainment figures in the forties and fifties.

Ava was born on Christmas Eve in Grabtown, outside Smithfield. On the day she was born, two cakes were made, a birthday tradition her beloved sister Beatrice (Bappie) carried on all through Ava's adult life.

She was the youngest of six children. Her father, Josh Gardner, raised cotton and bright-leaf tobacco. When she was still a baby, her father lost his farm, and subsequently became a tenant farmer. Because of poverty and stress, her mother, Mary, took her children and left Josh. She then ran a boardinghouse for schoolteachers. Ava was very poor as a child and was embarrassed at having to wear the same sweater to school every day. When she was 12, her father died.

She graduated from Rock Ridge High School in Rock Ridge and started studying stenography at Atlantic Christian College in Wilson. She excelled in her work, typing 120 words per minute. Then her life took a sudden and unexpected turn.

During a visit to her sister Beatrice in New York, her brother-in-law, Larry Tarr, photographed her and placed the photo in the window of his Fifth Avenue studio. The photo attracted the attention of an MGM agent, who asked her to come out to Hollywood for a screen test. Her protective mother, who was ill with cancer at the time, insisted Beatrice accompany Ava to California.

Ava had never acted and had a strong Southern accent.

Ava Gardner
Courtesy of the North Carolina Division of Archives and History

Marvin Schenck, in charge of talent for MGM at the time, remembered Ava's test: "She was clumsy and uneasy and we all wanted to go to bed with her." Louis B. Mayer pronounced, "She can't act. She can't talk. She's terrific."

By 1940, Gardner was in Hollywood, earning $50 a week at MGM, playing bit parts. Twenty films into her career she was named Hollywood's Most Promising Newcomer of the Year.

For the next several years, she lived in the Hollywood fast lane. Her personal life was soon making headlines. While she was a new actress on the MGM lot, Mickey Rooney met and fell in love with her. They married in 1942, but the marriage was short-lived.

Her second marriage was to bandleader Artie Shaw in 1945. Their marriage was an unhappy one.

The rising star in 1942

Courtesy of the North Carolina Division of Archives and History

By 1946, she was a leading young star. Over the next few years she starred in top movies such as *Pandora and the Flying Dutchman*; *The Snows of Kilimanjaro*; *Ride, Vaquero*, *Mogambo*; *Whistle Stop*; *The Killers*; *The Hucksters*; *The Sun Also Rises*; and *The Night of the Iguana*.

Her third marriage, to Frank Sinatra, took place in 1951 and lasted a few years.

The free-spirited Gardner continued to be the center of publicity, as well as the subject of fabricated and embellished stories, which sold movies. One writer mused in a *Saturday Evening Post* article in 1948: "The hussy-seeming Gardner the public meets in newspaper photos, rotogravure pages, Sunday-feature sections, and picture magazines is largely a creation of make-up, clever lighting, slick camera work, and gossip columnists striving to gratify their readers' wishful thinking."

Gardner left Hollywood for Spain in 1954 after boo-hooing its phoniness. In 1968, after a long stay in Madrid where she led a high-profile life, she moved to London, choosing a more subdued and tranquil existence.

Ava Gardner died of pneumonia on January 25, 1990, and was buried in Smithfield.

An Ava Gardner Museum has been established in Smithfield. Temporarily housed in the Austin Building on South Third Street, plans are underway to move the museum to a more permanent location when funds have been raised. The museum collection consists of memorabilia, school photos, film clips, film costumes, domestic and foreign film posters, scripts, scrapbooks, magazine covers, and other material.

SELECTED FILMS
Lost Angel, 1943
The Killers, 1946
Whistle Stop, 1946

The Hucksters, 1947
Show Boat, 1951
Pandora and the Flying Dutchman, 1951
The Snows of Kilimanjaro, 1952
Ride, Vaquero, 1953
Mogambo, 1953
The Sun Also Rises, 1957
The Night of the Iguana, 1964
Earthquake, 1974
City on Fire, 1979

SOURCES
The Saturday Evening Post, June 5, 1948, "Tar Heel Tornado," Pete Martin.
Newsweek, November 24, 1952, pgs. 93-98, unattributed.
Vanity Fair, June 1984, pgs. 16-18, Dominick Dunne.
Greensboro Daily News, December 17, 1972, Mal Vincent, North Carolina Collection clipping file through 1975, University of North Carolina at Chapel Hill Library.
Ava's Men, Jane Ellen Ward, St. Martin's Press, New York, 1990.
Ava Gardner, John Daniell, St. Martin's Press, New York, 1982.
Ava: My Story, Bantam, New York, 1990.

Kathryn Grayson
1921-

Kathryn Grayson is renowned as a film and stage performer, who has had leading roles in a variety of musicals, operas, and dramas including *Camelot*, *Show Boat*, and *Kiss Me Kate*.

Grayson was born Zelma Hedrick in Winston-Salem. Her family moved to St. Louis, Missouri when she was two, and she spent her childhood there. Grayson studied voice before training with Frances Marshall of the Chicago Civic Opera. She signed with RCA Red Seal Records when she was 15. She attended Los Angeles' Manual Art High School.

Just as her opera career was taking hold, she was seen by Louis B. Mayer at a music festival. She was signed by MGM without the formality of a screen test. Upon later viewing herself on screen, she said, "I was so awful on the screen, I tried to walk out several times."

Her unusual combination of looks, singing voice, and acting talent brought her stardom in 1943. A major star at MGM, Grayson also made films for Warner Brothers and Paramount. She had strong opinions about performing. "I don't want to do a musical that has songs suddenly coming out of the air for no reason," she said.

Her career has spanned film, television, dramatic, and musical stage performances. Her TV performances include *Playhouse 90* and *General Electric Theater*. She was nominated for an Emmy Award for Best Actress for *Shadow on the Heart*, a production of *General Electric Theater*.

It wasn't until 1960 that she returned to opera, making her debut performing *Madame Butterfly*, *La Traviata*, and *La Boheme*. In 1983, she starred in *Orpheus in the Underworld* for Opera New England.

Kathryn Grayson
Courtesy of Kathryn Grayson

Grayson continued to do other work. In 1982, she was favorably reviewed for her dramatic stage performance in Lucille Fletcher's *Night Watch*. In 1987, she appeared in the British farce, *Noises Off*, which brought more accolades for her acting ability. In 1988, she received the Albert Schweitzer Award which recognizes performing artists dedicated to music and devoted to humanity.

Kathryn Grayson has led and continues to lead an active life. She has twice married and divorced, and has a daughter. In 1991, she performed in a one-woman show, *An Evening with Kathryn Grayson* which contained everything from film clips to arias. Her singing voice is still quite good.

SELECTED FILMS
Andy Hardy's Private Secretary, 1941
The Vanishing Virginian, 1941
Rio Rita, 1941
Anchors Aweigh, 1945
Ziegfeld Follies, 1945
Show Boat, 1951
The Desert Song, 1953
Kiss Me Kate, 1954

SELECTED STAGE PERFORMANCES
Madame Butterfly, 1960
Something's Afoot, 1983
Noise Off, 1987

SOURCES
Biographical Information from Kathryn Grayson.
Celebrity Register, edited by Cleveland Amory, Harper & Row Publishers, New York, 1963.

Nina Simone
Courtesy of the Schomberg Center, New York Public Library

Nina Simone
1935-

Nina Simone won widespread recognition for her original brand of music in the late fifties. She has been dubbed the Queen of Shebang and the High Priestess of Soul because her style is a unique synthesis of African chants, gospel songs, work songs, blues, show tunes, protest songs, and ballads, some of her own composing.

She has been praised as well for her performance style no matter the size of the audience. She is a true performer in the sense that she captivates the audience, and is uninhibited. Consequently the performances are very intimate.

Nina Simone was born Eunice Kathleen Waymon on February 21, 1935 in Tryon, the sixth of eight children. Her father was a handyman and her mother a housekeeper and an ordained Methodist minister. Eunice grew up in poverty. The fact that she was black made her life difficult.

But she was talented. At the age of three, she was playing piano by ear, and by the time she was seven, she had attracted the attention of one of her mother's employers who paid for her piano lessons with a local teacher, Mrs. Lawrence Mazzanovich. After two years, she gave the lessons free.

The lessons led to recitals, which proved difficult emotionally for Eunice, but helped pave the way for future successes. Mazzanovich later established the "Eunice Waymon Fund," which was the savings from all of her pupil's performances.

Money provided by the fund enabled Eunice to attend Allen High School for Girls in Asheville, where she graduated in 1950, valedictorian of her class. She was also president of the student council, pianist for the glee club, member of the choir and basketball team, and an actress in school plays.

She suffered heartaches over many of her experiences in North Carolina. Growing up as a young black woman in the South, Eunice felt firsthand the bitter sting of bigotry.

After graduating high school, she attended the Julliard School of Music in New York. During that time, her family moved to Philadelphia to be closer to her. When the fund money ran out she returned to her family in Philadelphia. There she worked as a vocal trainer for $45 a week and continued her study of classical music.

In 1954, during a summer break from her job, she found work at the Midtown Bar in Atlantic City, New Jersey for $90 a week. The club's owner thought he was only hiring a vocalist, and wasn't aware she could also play the piano until the first night of her engagement. She sang and played and was an instant hit. She played the bar for three summers and gained a loyal following, particularly of college students.

During her run at the Midtown, Eunice Waymon changed her name to Nina Simone. When she was a kid she had been called "Nina," which means little girl in Spanish. She says "Simone" just seemed to make a good combination.

Her first commercial success was her recording of Gershwin's "I Love You Porgy," from *Porgy and Bess*, inspired by the classic Billie Holiday version. She was soon appearing in nightclubs such as the Village Gate, the Village Vanguard, the Embers, and the Roundtable, and concerts at the Newport Jazz Festival and Carnegie Hall. She also made appearances on television.

Simone proved to be an independent woman who didn't care if she made a scene. In December 1960, while working at the Village Gate, she helped precipitate a court case testing the constitutionality of the regulations covering the fingerprinting of New York City cabaret employees.

In a *New York Post* article in 1961, Edward Kosner said that Simone is "a member of a new breed of Negro entertainer—the antithesis of the posturing 'Uncle Tom' who would do anything to win an audience's approval...(While she) wants the approval of an audience desperately...that approval must come on *her* terms and be grounded in respect for her work."

In articles in *Time* and other magazines, Simone is said to be difficult to get along with and a moody performer, but many of those same critics see that behavior as what makes her such a strong performer. She is demanding of herself and her public, and creates a fresh relationship with each audience, certainly an emotionally exhausting feat.

Simone's first marriage, to Donald Ross, ended in divorce in 1960. In 1961, she married Andrew Benjamin Stroud, who quit his job as a detective sergeant in the New York City Police Force to become her manager and partner in the Rolls Royce Music Company, the Ninandy Music Company, and Stroud Productions and Enterprises, Inc.

Simone and her husband live in Mount Vernon, New York, with their daughter, Nina Celeste.

ALBUMS
Wild is the Wind
High Priestess of Soul
Silk & Soul
Pastel Blues
I Put a Spell On You
Let It All Out
Nina Simone Sings the Blues

SOURCES
Current Biography Yearbook 1968, pgs. 365-368, Charles Moritz, The H.W. Wilson Company, New York, 1968.
Encyclopedia of Jazz in the Sixties, pg. 262, Leonard Feather, Horizon Press, New York, 1966.
Encyclopedia of Jazz in the Seventies, pg. 308, Leonard Feather and Ira Gitler, Horizon Press, New York, 1976.
Redbook Magazine, November 1970, "High Priestess of Soul," Maya Angelou.

Kate Smith
1907-1986

Kate Smith, radio personality and patriotic symbol famed for her rendition of "God Bless America," had a singing career spanning almost 50 years. In 1979, she moved to Raleigh under unusual circumstances.

Smith first sang "God Bless America" on her radio show from New York on November 11, 1938, which is now known as Veteran's Day. At that time, Europe was on the brink of World War II, and Americans were still undecided about entering the conflict. The song became a kind of second national anthem, inspiring her nickname "radio's own Statue of Liberty."

In 1939, President Franklin D. Roosevelt introduced Smith to King George VI of England by saying, "This is Kate Smith—this is America."

Smith's singing of "God Bless America" helped generate $600 million worth of bond sales, while she traveled the country entertaining troops. The revenues continue to provide funds for the Boy Scouts of America.

In 1976, she went into a diabetic coma, and although she recovered, it left her confined to a wheelchair. In 1979, a New York court appointed Smith's attorney and her two nieces as conservators of her estate. The judge instructed them to sell Smith's New York apartment and other properties, and buy her a house in Raleigh where her sister, Helena Smith Steene, and nieces were living. The nieces returned to court several times to dispute the conservatorship. In 1979, Smith moved from Lake Placid, New York to Raleigh.

In 1982, President Ronald Reagan awarded Smith the Presidential Medal of Freedom, the highest honor for a civil-

Kate Smith

Courtesy of the North Carolina Collection, UNC at Chapel Hill Library

ian. Previous recipients include CBS News Anchorman Walter Cronkite, actor Kirk Douglas, and former Secretary of State Edmund S. Muskie. The recipients are selected directly by the president.

That same year, she appeared on the Emmy Awards with Bob Hope pushing her wheelchair, and she sang "God Bless America."

Smith died in 1986 after a long battle with diabetes and high blood pressure. For 17 months after her death, a debate over where and how she would be buried raged and made headlines. During that time, her body was stored in a vault in Lake Placid while church officials and family members argued over a clause in her will, which requested that Smith be interred at the St. Agnes Roman Catholic Church's graveyard, also in Lake Placid, "in a hermetically sealed bronze casket in a mausoleum sufficient to contain my remains alone."

Church rules forbade above-ground burials, but after long negotiations, the church relented in honor of its most famous parishioner. Smith had been a summer resident of Lake Placid since 1932 and had converted to Catholicism at St. Agnes in 1965.

On November 14, 1987, seven hundred fans attended a memorial mass for Smith at St. Agnes. Her body was finally interred in the specially built mausoleum off to one side of the cemetery.

SOURCES

Charlotte Observer, August 30, 1980, Jim Dumbell, North Carolina Collection, unbound, University of North Carolina at Chapel Hill Library.

The News and Observer, Raleigh, NC, December 25, 1984, Sharon Overton, North Carolina Collection, unbound, University of North Carolina at Chapel Hill Library.

The News and Observer, Raleigh, NC, June 18, 1986, Sharon

Overton and Kema Soderberg, North Carolina Collection, unbound, University of North Carolina at Chapel Hill Library. *The News and Observer*, Raleigh, NC, November 15, 1987, New York Times News Service, North Carolina Collection, unbound, University of North Carolina at Chapel Hill Library. *The News and Observer*, Raleigh, NC, February 27, 1981, Rick Warner, North Carolina Collection, unbound, University of North Carolina at Chapel Hill Library.

SCIENCE

Dr. Annie Lowrie Alexander
Courtesy of *The Charlotte Observer*—© 1991

Dr. Annie Lowrie Alexander
1864-1929

Dr. Annie Lowrie Alexander decided upon her profession when she was 13 years old. Her dream would take her many years of hard work—the kind of perseverance that few exhibit. In 1887, she became the first female physician to practice in the South.

Born near the town of Cornelius in Mecklenburg County, she was the daughter of Dr. John Brevard Alexander, a physician and author, and Ann Wall Lowrie. Her father and a private tutor provided her early education.

She studied medicine at the Women's Medical College of Philadelphia, graduating from that institution in 1884. She followed her studies with a year-long internship there, and subsequently became an assistant teacher of anatomy in the Women's Medical College of Baltimore, while at the same time working in private practice.

In 1885, she obtained her license from the Maryland Board of Medical Examiners. In a class of 100 candidates, in which she was the only woman, she made the highest grade.

Two years later, Dr. Alexander moved to Charlotte, earning a reputation as a highly competent doctor, despite the fact that many still believed women shouldn't work as physicians.

Now there are myriad specialties within the field of medicine, but that wasn't the case when "Doctor Annie" was practicing. She was responsible for all areas of her patients' care.

In 1890, she moved to 410 North Tryon Street with her

parents. The one-story frame house had a stable in the back for her horse, her partner in many a long drive through the town and country.

For many years, her work included staff positions with Presbyterian and St. Peter's Hospitals in Charlotte. Dr. Alexander served as president of the Mecklenburg County Medical Society and vice-president of the Women Physicians of the Southern Medical Association. She was also an honorary member of the North Carolina Medical and Southern Medical Associations. She died in 1929.

SOURCES

Charlotte Observer, October 16, 1929, unattributed, North Carolina Collection clipping file through 1975, University of North Carolina at Chapel Hill Library.

Charlotte Observer, January 21, 1940, LeGette Blythe, North Carolina Collection clipping file through 1975, University of North Carolina at Chapel Hill Library.

Dictionary of North Carolina Biography, Volume One, pg. 13, Harold J. Dudley, edited by William S. Powell, The University of North Carolina Press, Chapel Hill, NC, 1979.

Dr. Susan Dimock
1847-1875

Dr. Susan Dimock overcame the barriers faced by the women of her time, becoming the first woman from North Carolina to practice medicine. Although she died when she was only 28, her impact as a pioneer was significant.

The obstacles of her time included public ridicule. As late as 1871, the same year she graduated from medical school, the president of the American Medical Association, Alfred Stille, argued that women were "unfitted by nature" to become physicians or other professionals because of their "uncertainty of rational judgment, capriciousness of sentiment, fickleness of purpose, and indecision of action."

Susan was born in Washington, North Carolina on April 24, 1847. Her father was Henry Dimock, originally from Limington, Maine, a headmaster and later the editor of *The North State Whig*, a local newspaper. Her mother was Mary Malvina Owens of Washington, who taught school and managed a local hotel, the Lafayette, which the couple purchased and resided in.

Her mother provided Susan's schooling at the hotel. At first she was her mother's only pupil, then other young women joined her in learning. She showed an early fascination with medicine and was fortunate to have two physicians from whom she was able to learn. One was her paternal grandfather and the other was the family physician, Dr. Solomon Satchwell. Both were sources of medical knowledge and stories. Latin became her favorite subject, and she spent hours translating prescriptions from an old Latin pharmacology book which belonged to Dr. Satchwell.

When Dimock was about 17, her father died. As her town

Dr. Susan Dimock
Courtesy of the North Carolina Collection, UNC at Chapel Hill Library

had been under occupation by Union soldiers for two years, culminating in the burning of the Lafayette Hotel, she and her mother moved to Massachusetts and lived with an aunt. Shortly afterward, she got a job as a teacher in Hopkinton, Massachusetts.

Though she had to temporarily put aside her goal of attending medical school for more immediate demands, Dimock didn't forget her dream. She continued to read voraciously, and as luck would have it, a friendship helped her realize her goal.

Bessie Greene, the daughter of wealthy Bostonian, Colonel Greene, became a close friend. The colonel was fascinated by Dimock's desire to become a physician. He helped her contact Dr. Marie Zakrezewska, a Pole, who had come to the United States with the help of Dr. Elizabeth Blackwell, the first woman doctor in this country. Dr. Zakrezewska gave Susan a list of medical books to study. Dimock later applied and was admitted as a student at the New England Hospital for Women and Children in Boston, Massachusetts.

Dimock was ambitious and persistent. A year later, wanting to broaden her experiences, she applied to Harvard University, which promptly refused her entrance. Massachusetts General Hospital, on the other hand, accepted her—with the provision that she attend on different days than the regular medical students.

Unwilling to accept such treatment, she decided to attend the University of Zurich instead. She received a medical degree with honors in 1871. After that, she studied at hospitals in Vienna and Paris, and in 1872, the North Carolina Medical Society made her an honorary member. Dimock returned to the states and began working as a resident physician at the New England Hospital for Women and Children.

After three years, her career was well underway. She asked for a five-month leave to study abroad and vacation. On April 27, 1875, she left New York with Bessie Greene and

Caroline Crane aboard the *Schiller*, considered one of the best of the great iron-rigged steam ships of the day.

Two weeks later, the ship, navigating through dense fog, crashed into a granite reef 25 miles off the coast of Cornwall, England. Most of the passengers, including Dimock and her two companions, died. Colonel Greene arranged to have the bodies of his daughter and her friends brought to Boston where they were interred in Forest Hills Cemetery.

For weeks afterward, the international press wrote passionate tributes to Susan Dimock, pioneer woman doctor.

MAJOR WORKS

"The Different Forms of Puerperal Fever" (dissertation—circa 1871)

SOURCES

Memoir of Susan Dimock, Resident Physician of the New England Hospital for Women and Children, 1875, North Carolina Collection, University of North Carolina at Chapel Hill Library.

The News and Observer, Raleigh, NC, May 16, 1920, unattributed, North Carolina Collection clipping file through 1975, University of North Carolina at Chapel Hill Library.

Dictionary of North Carolina Biography, Volume Two, pg. 70, Pauline Worthy, edited by William S. Powell, The University of North Carolina Press, Chapel Hill, NC, 1986.

Tar Heel Women, Lou Rogers, Warren Publishing Company, Raleigh, NC, 1949.

Gertrude B. Elion
1918-

Gertrude B. Elion has received the Nobel Prize for medicine, has received ten honorary doctoral degrees from prestigious institutions such as Brown University, and was the first woman elected to the National Inventors Hall of Fame. A researcher for Burroughs Wellcome for nearly 50 years, Elion has worked at Research Triangle Park for more than two decades.

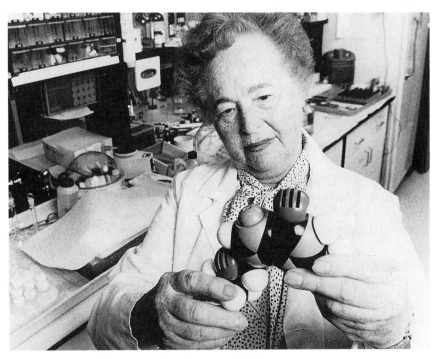

Dr. Gertrude B. Elion
Courtesy of Burroughs Wellcome

Elion speaks with insight, wit, and honesty, and it is easy to understand why this woman is a survivor in a system which might easily gobble up those less hearty. Elion is part of the scientific bastion, a traditionally white male enclave where women were once shunned, but of late have carved themselves a growing niche.

Dr. Elion in 1952

Courtesy of Burroughs Wellcome

Elion was born on January 23, 1918, in New York City. When she was 15 her grandfather died of cancer, and she recalls being horrified by what the disease did to this man she loved so much. This experience helped to catalyze her future. She did well in high school and headed for college. Because of her experience with her grandfather's disease, she focused on cancer research.

"I hadn't ever really thought it might be difficult for a woman to do cancer research," she says matter-of-factly. In 1937, at the age of 19, she graduated from Hunter College with an A.B. in chemistry, summa cum laude and Phi Beta Kappa. Then she met with a dose of reality.

"Being a woman was a real disadvantage early on in my career," she says. "Some people told me, 'we've never had a woman in the lab; we think you'll be a distracting influence. You'll get married and leave'—the old cliche of women belong at home."

What she wanted to do was get into the research lab, but what she had to do for several years was suffer through "a lot of mediocre jobs." At first she worked as an unpaid laboratory assistant. After six months, she was put on the payroll. She taught high school chemistry and physics for two years while completing research for a master's degree in chemistry from New York University, which she received in 1941.

One of her first jobs was as a food analyst in a laboratory. Her job consisted of checking the acidity of the pickles and making sure the berries, which were going into jam, were not moldy.

The opportunity to get her foot in the proverbial door came in the guise of World War II. Millions of men joined the war effort, which left a desperate need for workers at home. Finally the work force welcomed women. Many employers considered the phenomenon temporary, but many women including Elion, once in, were there to stay.

In 1944, she joined the Wellcome Research Laboratories in Research Triangle Park, a research-based pharmaceutical company where she worked as a biochemist and assistant to Dr. George Hitchings. For Elion and Hitchings, this was the beginning of a 30 year research collaboration.

The type of work they were engaged in was not particularly glamorous. According to Elion, "Drug research is a slow and cumulative process. There are many hurdles to overcome— synthesizing the compound, testing it in vitro, in animals, in humans, watching even after approval for unexpected bene- fits and unwanted side effects. There aren't many eureka moments."

A highlight for her was giving her first paper at a major meeting. It was in the late forties or early fifties. After presenting the paper, she fielded questions from the audi- ence. "The person who questioned me was a brilliant bio- chemist who worked for the Rockefeller Institute, Wayne Woolley. I didn't know who he was and he questioned me, and I stood my ground. Afterwards, they (her colleagues) said, 'Do you know who you were arguing with?'"

After the session she had lunch with Woolley. They talked

more about the interpretation of her drug test results, and she left palpably bolstered by the encounter.

She was later promoted to senior research chemist and assistant to the research director. In 1967, she was appointed head of the Department of Experimental Therapy, a position she held until 1983 when she retired and became scientist emeritus.

In 1984, following the principles of Hitchings and Elion, Burroughs Wellcome researchers developed the AIDS drug zidovudine (AZT).

In 1988, Elion was one of three scientists awarded the Nobel Prize in physiology or medicine, in recognition of her pioneering work in developing medications to treat some of mankind's most significant diseases. This award is typically given to academic scientists and not those involved in the pharmaceutical industry. The prize was awarded almost 30 years after most of the team's discoveries.

In 1991, she was the first woman elected to the National Inventors Hall of Fame. Begun in 1973, it was founded and dedicated to the individuals who have conceived technological advances fostered by the United States patent system. Elion says, "To those of us looking for new cures for serious medical problems, patents are an insurance policy for the protection of the investment in research."

In addition to being a scientist emeritus, she is research professor of Pharmacology and Medicine at Duke University and adjunct professor of Pharmacology at the University of North Carolina at Chapel Hill. She has been an active member of research and professional organizations including the American Association for Cancer Research and Council for Research and Clinical Investigation of the American Cancer Society. She has received numerous honors, degrees, appointments, and lectureships.

Asked about her thoughts on marriage and career, she says, "I think they (women) can have both, but they have to have a husband who understands both aspects of a woman's life...You can have a great deal of both worlds."

Elion was engaged once, but her fiancé died of subacute bacterial endocarditis. It took her a long time to get over his death, and though she had other friends, she never married or had children.

She reflects on the changes she has seen in her field. "I think there are a lot more women doing work in chemistry, which was very rare in my day."

"The place where discrimination still occurs is...at the top, (the) glass ceiling. They'll let you become a department head, (but) even though you're handling fifty-five people, they still don't think of you as a high administrator...My reaction is I'd rather be a scientist than a vice-president, but if I wanted to be one, why couldn't I?"

DRUGS DEVELOPED
mercaptopurine (leukemia treatment)
thioguanine (leukemia treatment)
Imuran (reduces likelihood of kidney rejection after kidney transplant)
allopurinol (gout and kidney stone treatment)
acyclovir (therapy for herpes virus infections)

SOURCES
Telephone interview with Dr. Gertrude B. Elion on July 23, 1991.
Press information from Burroughs Wellcome Company, October 1988-March 1991.
The New York Times Magazine, January 29, 1989, "The Nobel Pair," Katherine Bouton.

Maggie Axe Wachacha
Courtesy of *The Cherokee One Feather*

Maggie Axe Wachacha
1894-

Most facets of Maggie Axe Wachacha are not easily defined. Wachacha is a Cherokee Indian who has been acknowledged for her work by her own tribe, as well as the state of North Carolina.

In 1978, the Western Band of Cherokees of Oklahoma held a joint council with the Eastern Band of Cherokees of North Carolina. It was the first meeting since the Trail of Tears, when Cherokees from North Carolina, Georgia, and Tennessee were forcibly removed to Oklahoma in the summer of 1838. At the council, Wachacha was given the title "Beloved Woman," considered the most prestigious title granted by the people of the two Cherokee nations. Traditionally given to the widowed wife of the Principal Chief, Wachacha was given the title because of her work as an herbalist, midwife, and tribal clerk.

In 1986, Wachacha was one of five to receive the North Carolina Distinguished Women Award from Governor Jim Martin. Ninety-one women had been nominated by individuals and organizations across the state.

When I interviewed Wachacha, she was seated in a wheelchair on the porch of the modest home built for her by the tribe. Two dogs, two kittens, and several roosters and hens wandered around us. Wachacha wore a housecoat because her guest came later than planned and she had been napping. Her face was creased with deep lines, but it was a kind face, and she smiled easily.

She was surrounded by family members. Abe, her thirtyish grandson, whom she helped raise, and his wife Renee were seated and occasionally clarified questions or answers.

Wachacha's daughter, Winnona, was there with her husband, Mac Reed, who was the first translator. Great-grandson Damien was curled up in Abe and Renee's pick-up truck.

The adults joked and talked in Cherokee and then quickly and easily switched to English. Wachacha was equally conversant in both languages, but as of late she preferred her native tongue, allowing one of her family members to translate her words.

Wachacha is 97—if you follow tribal records. She was born on September 16, 1894, at Snowbird Gap, not far from her current home a few miles outside of Robbinsville, to Will and Caroline Cornsilk Axe.

The language always spoken in her home was Cherokee. She taught herself to write it at home when she was seven years old, using chalk or writing in the dirt. Sometimes her father read it to her and she would write it in chalk on a slab of slate rock. Her father told her that one day she would go to Cherokee and work, and this provided an incentive to learn.

She attended a one-room, English-speaking school four months out of the year, when it was either too cold to work or when there was no work to be done. She stopped attending after the fourth grade. Her English began with the words "Jesus Christ," and the rest came easily from listening to people talk. Though she was not extensively trained in English or Cherokee, she is fluent and literate in both.

In 1935, she met and married Jarrett Wachacha, who died in 1974 at the age of 101. They built a cabin just up the road from where she lives now. Winnona, their only child, was born a year later.

Wachacha has been recognized by many for her achievements, but when asked what she was most proud of, she quickly responded, her work as a healer. This included herbal healing. Her grandmother taught her about the healing power of roots and where to get them. A common problem she dealt with through herbal medicine was diabetes. She said it was easily cured with four treatments of sassafrass. Other health problems she treated included headaches and gall stones. Sometimes her patients paid her in clothes, groceries, and snuff which she used until about two years ago. She said she could write a book on all of her medicines.

Wachacha was also a midwife, learning this skill from an aunt who was a well-regarded midwife. From the age of ten, she was at her aunt's side, helping Cherokee mothers through the birthing process. As an adult, she assisted in the delivery of over 3,000 babies. She mentioned the names of several people she delivered: Shirley Oswald, Emily Wachacha, and her last, twenty-five years ago, Hettie Bird, her granddaughter. She said she quit delivering when she heard they were going to start locking up midwives.

Though she has given up midwifery and healing, several of her relatives added that people still come to her for herbal treatments. "Yeah, they still come," she said.

Beginning in 1937, Wachacha served as the Tribal Indian Clerk for the Eastern Band of Cherokee Indians. An annual meeting was held in the fall for three days, entirely in the Cherokee language. She walked the 30 mile trip with her husband Jarrett, an elected councilman from Snowbird Township. It took them two days to walk from the mountains of Snowbird to Cherokee.

At the meeting, her duties included transcribing the minutes into the Sequoyian Syllabary, the written language of the Cherokee which was developed more than 160 years ago.

In addition to her work as a healer and clerk, she has spent many hours teaching. She taught the Cherokee Indian class at Zion Hill Baptist Church for many years and also taught reading and writing in Cherokee at the elementary and high school levels.

SOURCES

Interview with Maggie Axe Wachacha on August 7, 1991 (translated by Mac Reed and Abe Wachacha).

Information from Abe Wachacha, Renee Wachacha, and Richard Welch.

The Cherokee One Feather, Cherokee, NC, April 19, 1978, Rich Welch.

Winston-Salem Journal, August 24, 1986, Frank Tursi.

The Atlanta Journal and Constitution, November 30, 1986, Ron Martz.

Journal of Cherokee Studies: Fading Voices, Special Edition, Museum of the Cherokee Indian, Cherokee Communications, Cherokee, NC, 1991.

The Cherokee One Feather, Cherokee, NC, March 26, 1986, Gill Jackson.

REFORM

Penelope Barker
Courtesy of the North Carolina Collection, UNC at Chapel Hill Library

Penelope Barker
1728-1796

Penelope Barker was an outspoken defender of colonists' rights in the years before the American Revolution. She became famous for orchestrating what is known as the Edenton Tea Party, a group of 51 women who gathered to formally protest unfair taxation imposed by Great Britain.

Barker's was a long hard life which reached its public peak with that act. She was born in Edenton in Chowan County, to Samuel Padgett, physician and planter, and Elizabeth Blount. They raised their daughter as a member of high society.

While Penelope was still in her teens, her father and married sister, Elizabeth, died, and she took responsibility for her sister's household, including three children. A few years later, she married her sister's widower, John Hodgson, and they had two sons. He died a few years later.

A widow at nineteen, she remarried four years later. Her marriage to James Craven, a local planter and political leader, was brief as he also died soon after. He bequeathed his entire estate to her.

A couple of years later, she married Thomas Barker, an Edenton attorney and member of the assembly. They had three children, none of whom lived to one year of age. In 1761, she was left alone to manage the household and plantations when her husband sailed for London to serve as agent for the North Carolina colony.

On October 25, 1774, fifty-one women met for a tea party at the home of Elizabeth King, wife of an Edenton merchant. However, on this occasion, there was one crucial difference; they refused to imbibe any tea, following Penelope Barker's lead. For the American colonists, the tea party was an important social event, similar to the British model. The highlight of Barker's meeting was the penning of a letter which expressed their dissatisfaction with Parliament's Tea Act of 1773.

It stated: "We the ladyes of Edenton do hereby solemnly engage not to conform to ye pernicious Custom of Drinking Tea or that we, the aforesaid Ladyes, will not promote ye wear of any manufacture from England, until such time that all Acts which tend to enslave this our Native Country shall be repealed."

Wanting more than a local audience for their views, the women sent copies of the letter to England, where the names of all 51 were published in the newspaper.

As a result of the American Revolution and the British blockade of American ports, Thomas Barker was forced to remain in England until early September, 1778.

He died in 1789 and Penelope died in 1796. Both were buried at Hays Plantation near Edenton.

In 1975, Susan Graham Ervin wrote and produced *Oh, Penelope!,* a musical which chronicles the Edenton Tea Party. The only known portrait of Penelope Barker hangs in the Cupola House in Edenton.

SOURCES
Dictionary of North Carolina Biography, Volume One, pg. 95, Michael G. Martin, Jr., edited by William S. Powell, The University of North Carolina Press, Chapel Hill, NC, 1979.
Charlotte Observer, October 9, 1975, Pat Borden.
Tar Heel Women, Lou Rogers, Warren Publishing Company, Raleigh, NC, 1949.

Dorothea Dix
1802-1887

Although Dorothea Dix was not born in North Carolina and never lived in the state, she made a lasting impact on the Tar Heel state during the time she spent here. Dix was a champion of the mentally ill, and her legacy in North Carolina is Dorothea Dix Hospital in Raleigh, the state hospital for the mentally ill.

Dix was one of many Europeans and Americans involved in a movement during the late 18th and early 19th centuries to improve both working and living conditions for the working class. Along with improved conditions in factories, these reformers also worked for free public schools, and increased women's rights.

Dix labored to improve the lives of the mentally ill. Her work had an impact in both the United States and Europe, but it took many years and struggles for her plans to come to fruition.

Dix was born in southern Maine in a one-room cottage to Joseph and Mary (Bigelow) Dix. Her father was described as a nervous and moody man who left Harvard College at 19 to marry her mother, a sickly woman. Dorothea's immediate family consisted of two brothers, whose company she enjoyed, but in general her early years were not happy.

One of Dorothea's early pleasures was spending time with her paternal grandparents in Boston. They had more time and money to spend with her than her parents. Dr. Elijah Dix took his granddaughter on calls with him and taught her to read from books in his library. When her grandfather died, she moved in with her grandmother, a fortunate turn of events for Dorothea.

At age 14, she was teaching school in Worcester, Massachusetts. In 1821, she established the Dix Mansion in Boston, a school for young girls. The core of the curriculum was the building of moral character. The natural sciences were also strongly emphasized. During those years, Dix wrote a number of books.

She overworked herself and became ill. Her doctor suggested she visit his friends, the Rathbones, in England. She followed his advice and left. It took his friends 18 months to nurse her back to health. While in England, she met Samuel Tuke, a doctor in charge of a home for insane people. At York Retreat, contrary to popular belief, Tuke was able to cure some of his mentally ill patients.

In 1841, back in the U.S., Dix began work as a Sunday school teacher for women prisoners in the East Cambridge House of Corrections in Massachusetts. On her first day she found a group of women in an unheated room. The criminals and mentally ill had been put together. Several times she requested the room be heated and the women separated, but to no avail.

Angry and frustrated by the lack of response, Dix began the work which would bring about change. For 18 months, she toured Massachusetts institutions where the mentally ill were confined. Shocked by the conditions she found, she wrote a report to the state legislature. She cited instances of patients confined in cages, closets, cellars, and pens. They were chained, some naked and some beaten with rods. The legislature, sufficiently impressed by the claims, instigated changes.

After her successful work in Massachusetts, she began doing similar investigative work in other states. She helped change laws and get separate hospitals for the mentally ill.

In North Carolina, Dix seemed to come at just the right time. Her gutsiness and determination proved the right combination to get things done.

Demands for a separate facility for the mentally ill were

Dorothea Dix
Courtesy of the North Carolina Division of Archives and History

first voiced in 1828. Governor after governor recommended the establishment of such a facility, but none was successful in rallying legislative support. So in 1848, when Dix came to lobby for a separate hospital, as well as more humane treatment for the mentally ill, the stage was set.

Because she was a woman working on political issues, she had to work through others. Governor William A. Graham commended her cause to the legislature, but the Whigs and Democrats, who had equal strength in both houses, didn't want to risk their popularity by voting away their constituents' money.

Dix invited some leading Democrats to call on her at the Mansion House, a Raleigh hotel, where she was staying. She turned to John W. Ellis, placed her memorial in his hands and said, "I desire you sir to present it...and you, gentlemen, you I expect will sustain the motion this gentleman will present to print the same."

Her memorial began:

> I appear as the advocate of those who cannot plead their own cause; I come as the friend of those who are deserted, oppressed, and desolate. In the Providence of God, I am the voice of the maniac whose piercing cries from the dreary dungeons of your jails penetrate not your Halls of Legislature. I am the Hope of the poor crazed beings who pine in the cells, and I am the Revelation of hundreds of wailing, suffering creatures, hidden in your private dwellings, and in pens and cabins—shut out, cut off from all healing influences, from all mind-restoring cares.

In 1848, a bill calling for the establishment of a special hospital for the mentally ill was defeated in the House because no funding source was found. However, a twist of fate later occurred, when James C. Dobbin, who would normally not be in favor of such a bill, was unable to attend the debate on the bill because he was at his wife's deathbed. As it turned out, Dix had been tending to his wife. One of his wife's dying requests was that he work for passage of the bill. He did so and it became law on January 1, 1849.

But it was seven years before the hospital would be ready for patients. On March 5, 1856, the hospital was ready to receive 40 patients, and a month later 40 more. By the end of the year, the hospital housed 90 patients; the causes of insanity were listed as: unknown-47, epilepsy-11, ill-health-8, and the rest were attributed to such miscellaneous causes as intemperance, masturbation, political excitement, and family troubles.

It occurred to Dix that both federal and state governments should help pay for the facilities, and so she stayed in Washington, D.C. four years, lobbying a bill which finally passed by a majority vote in both houses of Congress. The bill went to President Franklin Pierce, but he refused to sign it. He said states should care for their own poor and handicapped, not the federal government.

During the Civil War, Dix was appointed Superintendent of United States Army Nurses, in charge of choosing nurses for the Union Army. Louisa May Alcott, author of *Little Women*, was one of the nurses she chose. Alcott later wrote *Hospital Sketches* about that experience.

Dorothea Dix Hospital in Raleigh is still functioning as an institution for the mentally ill.

BOOKS

Conversations on Common Things, 1824
Evening Hours, 1825
Meditations for Private Hours, 1828
The Garland of Flora, 1829

The Pear, or Affection's Gift; a Christmas and New Year's Present, 1829
Ten Short Stories for Children, 1827 (republished as *American Moral Tales for Young Persons*, 1832)
Hymns for Children, Selected and Altered, 1825

SOURCES

Dictionary of American Biography, Volume Three, pgs. 323-325, edited by Allen Johnson and Dumas Malone, Charles Scribner's Sons, New York, 1958.
Memorial Soliciting a State Hospital for the Protection and Cure of the Insane, Dorothea Dix, 1848.
The North Carolina Historical Review, Volume XIII, Number 3, pgs. 185-201, Margaret Callender McCulloch, July 1936.
Four Women of Courage, Mary Malone, edited by Bennett Wayne, Garrard Publishing Company, Champaign, IL, 1975.

INDEX